# The Sustainers: Citizens of the United States

# THE SUSTAINERS: CITIZENS OF THE UNITED STATES

by
William T. Mayton

TWELVE TABLES PRESS
XII

www.twelvetablespress.com

P.O. Box 568
Northport, New York 11768

Library of Congress Cataloging-in-Publication Data

Name: William T. Mayton, author
Title: The Sustainers, Citizens of the United States
Description: Northport, New York: Twelve Tables Press, 2017
ISBN 978-1-946074-02-7 (print)/ISBN 978-1-946074-03-4 (ebook)
Subjects: Law — United States/Constitution — United States/History
LC record available at https://lccn.loc.gov

Twelve Tables Press, LLC
P.O. Box 568
Northport, New York 11768
Telephone (631) 241-1148
Fax (631) 754-1913
www.twelvetablespress.com

Printed in the United States of America

# Table of Contents

# Prologue

# "Seventeen Hundred Levelers with Firearms"

By his letter of June 24, 1826, Thomas Jefferson declined the invitation to attend the fiftieth-anniversary celebration of the document — the Declaration of Independence — he had written. He was in bad health and ten days later, on the day of that anniversary, July 4, he died. His letter included this statement, "the mass of mankind has not been born with saddles on their backs, nor a favored few booted and spurred, ready to ride them legitimately, by the grace of God." With those words, Jefferson recalled and repeated the last statement of an old Leveler, Col. Richard Rumbold, who delivered it from the gallows on which he was hanged by the English Crown for treason. For Rumbold, the terms of the metaphor — saddled, booted, and spurred — were a natural form of expression; he had been a cavalryman. As to the spirit of the message, as a Leveler he lived and died for that. I mention these things because the Levelers in a roundabout way led to this book.

The Levelers were a force during England's Civil War in the late 1640s, marked as they were by the sea green ribbons they wore and by the prose and passion of their cause. They held a notion of rights, of identified spaces of liberty held by an individual and as held secured from taking, by the king or any arm of the state. They carried a statement of their cause, the "Agreement of the People." But that movement failed. It led to a military protectorate followed by a restoration of the English Crown in the person of Charles II.

In the United States, the Levelers have had an appeal, on thoughts that our own Constitution is considerably owed to their "Agreement of the People" and that the leveling of our own society, as gained by our (successful) revolution, started with them. I was taken by those thoughts and spent

1

two years going through English sources. But then I turned back to us, to find that my preceding two years, at least in terms of usefully publishable work, were fruitless. In terms of what the Levelers might have brought to the table, for us that table had already been set. By the mid-seventeenth century, the foundation of our own and successful revolt, our leveling, was already in place.

So what was it, the groundwork we began in North America? It was a basis not yet understood in Great Britain and there would not be for another two hundred years. For us, though, the work started at Plymouth when the Pilgrims landed in 1620, the Mayflower Compact being evidence of the fact. At Jamestown, the work took a decade to form, but it did and was in place in 1618. Then in 1776 that movement, as had spread to the rest of colonies, became the Revolution.

At the start of the Revolutionary War, a British loyalist in New York spoke of a disturbance there by "seventeen hundred Levelers with fire-arms." But those armed people had come together under a different name. They were, as they said, "citizens" and fought for that order.

*The word they used, the citizen, was new.* We conceived it, the citizen, in 1776 and in that year used it for the first time in a public document, the Declaration of Independence. Then and now the citizen is an embedded fact. The British statesman who in time understood that fact, of the citizen, was Edmund Burke. During our resistance to Great Britain, Burke was sympathetic to our cause and famously expressed that sentiment in Parliament. What he then spoke of was our regard for "liberty" and "rights" — England should respect these claims rather than trying to crush them. But in the 1770s, Burke did not yet have the word for us. The word we had invented, the citizen, he not know. Fifteen years or so later the French Revolution came on, to which Burke was not at all sympathetic, and now he had the word, citizen, to show his hostility. In *Reflections on the French Revolution* (1790), he wrote, "In all societies, consisting of various descriptions of citizens, some description must be uppermost." The problem in the French Revolution, where *citoyen* was the salutation, was that the word was unhinged. Now it was used, Burke said, to "change and pervert the natural order of things . . . setting up in the air what the solidity of the structure requires to be on the ground." Burke saw the absence of the citizen and understood the consequences, guillotine and all.

The word we conceived in 1776, the citizen, is a noun that is both general and particular. A particularity, which *The Sustainers* is about, is the route to being a citizen.

# Chapter One

# Introduction

Civic disaggregation: The "gradual transformation
of the citizen-members of the civic order into a randomly
associated mass of individuals."

Selbourne, *The Principle of Duty:*
*An Essay on the Foundations of the Civic Order*

For a republic the citizen is crucial — much as an atom of carbon, given its capacity to bind, is essential to life on this planet. The affinities of the citizen, no less natural, one to another and then to the nation, are several. A short list, though, includes qualities of cooperation and commitment one to another and then to the polity in which they gather. The list includes contribution, so as to produce a stock of public goods, such as education and defense, and a social insurance that spreads risks, such as disability, across the whole society. Also, it includes the ability of citizens — the "we the people" denoted in our Constitution rather than *The Leviathan* — to identify and restrain bad actors and actions by establishing the rule and protection of law.

These capacities of a citizen are an evolved feature of a human being. But as well, the whole fruition of a citizen is culturally aided, as by education and upbringing. A republic must nurture all these parts, these capacities, as best it can. Should the citizenry disintegrate as these parts fail, the polity may not necessarily die but it will no longer be democratic, as we have always known. On the last day of the constitutional convention, as Benjamin Franklin was leaving Independence Hall, a lady outside the Hall asked him, "Well Doctor, what have we got a republic or a monarchy?" Franklin's reply was "A republic if you can keep it." However well we remember this better than two centuries later, we are unclear about a central part. A republic entails a body of keepers and these keepers are its citizens. What we today do not know, not in full, is this: Who are they, the citizen, and are they acquired in the first place?

We become a citizen in two ways — primarily by birth and secondarily by naturalization. By the Fourteenth Amendment of 1868, birthright citizenship is the main way. The secondary way, naturalization, comes out of immigration and Article I of the Constitution. For the moment, let me first of all speak of naturalization.

# Naturalization

For citizenship gained by naturalization: Standards are set by Congress and only by that body. The Constitution, in Article I, Section 8, places the matter of naturalization solely in Congress. As naturalized persons become citizens, the relevant standards are made by Congress and are published as federal statutes. As published, these standards now require moral character and civic competency gained by a period of living lawfully, a time of residency, among us. They require a demonstrated knowledge of our institutions and history, a working fluency in English, and then an oath of allegiance.

In 1790 our first Congress assumed its constitutional role of admitting immigrates and setting standards for their naturalization as a citizen. James Madison, a member of that body and same as that body at large, wished to encourage immigration and to enact legislation toward that end. Madison and the Congress thought that immigration should be directed only to those who would be, in their words, "good citizens." Toward that end, of good citizens, commitment counted, whether, as Madison said, a person "really meant to incorporate himself into our society." The well-intentioned person whom we thus welcomed was contrasted with those whom we might refer today to as free riders, those here in pursuit of nothing more than short-term personal gain. (Or as then said, as "leeches" that "stick to us until they get fill of our best blood, then fall off and leave us.") Virtue, as in "decency and propriety of conduct" of course, counted, as did "republican" character.

In particular, republican character was defined by what it was not. It was not the backward, servile, class-ordered mentality — the "sensations, impregnated with prejudices of education acquired under monarchical and aristocratic governments" — associated with Europe. In terms of what republican character was, references were to dispositions useful in a polity formed for the common good, as in "habits of temperate discussion, patient reasoning, and a capacity of enduring contradiction."

As gaining the good citizen was the norm set in 1790 for naturalization, it is so today. As naturalization ends with an oath of citizenship, it is a celebration of a privilege earned, a great day in the new citizen's life and in our collective life as a nation.

# Birthright Citizenship

However, as considerable as naturalization is to gaining the citizenship of our republic, it is not the primary source for citizens. Today, and by the Fourteenth Amendment, birthright citizenship is the source. One reason for this is numbers: While perhaps 650,000 people come here as immigrants and are naturalized as citizens, another huge number, four million or so, become citizens by a different route; they are born here as citizens. If for no reason other than this size, the four million born here each year, birthright citizenship is by the main and moving force of citizens, the river that carries us forward. It establishes an aggregate of persons fit enough to sustain a republic.

But unlike citizenship as gained by naturalization, where we do have a good idea of how and when a person becomes a citizen, *today we have no such understanding about birthright citizenship*. Not really.

Here is a modern example of a bad understanding of who is born as a citizen and who is not. During fighting in Afghanistan in 2003, Yaser Esam Hamdi, AK 47 in hand, surrendered to Afghan forces allied with the United States. Interrogation showed that he had been with the Taliban as an enemy combatant. He was detained at Guantanamo Bay and then in a brig at Charlestown. But with regard to that detention, Hamdi had what seemed a trump card. To be sure, he was a national of Saudi Arabia. He had lived and been raised there until he left for Afghanistan, and the Taliban, at age 20.

In 1989, however, Hamdi's parents were in Baton Rouge, Louisiana, on temporary visas under which his father worked on a project for Exxon. In that year, Hamdi was born there. Shortly after his birth his parents returned to Saudi Arabia, where Hamdi was brought up as a Saudi, without returning to or having any affiliation with the United States. Be that as it may, Hamdi, owing to his birth in Louisiana during his parent's brief stay there, claimed to be a US citizen. That being the case, he contested his detention in court.

In the courts Hamdi's citizenship was avoided but no findings were made. But that evasion slipped over some problems: Had he in fact been a citizen and had he gone over to the Taliban, had he not breached a citizen's duty of loyalty? Was not treason (giving aid and comfort to the enemy) an appropriate charge against him? It had been for Tomoya Kawakita, a US citizen who during World War II had joined Japan and its cause. At war's end he had been apprehended and charged with mistreating US prisoners of war (POWs) whom he had guarded. For those same acts other Japanese guards went unpunished. But because he was a US citizen, Kawakita was subject to a citizen's duty of loyalty, for breach of which he was convicted of treason and sentenced to death.[1]

By that measure, should not Hamdi have been charged with treason? If he was a citizen, then should he be charged with treason? I think not. Kawakita, as said by the courts in his case, had been "numbered with us." He had lived "his life among us; had been fed by our land; had been nurtured by our institutions; had enjoyed the privileges of American citizenship." Consequently, Kawakita was fairly subject to at times, and certainly for him, terrible duty of loyalty. On the other hand, a person of only a slight connection with a nation, as was the case with Hamdi, is not fairly imprinted with that duty, as had been Kawakita, or fairly subject to the penalty for violating it. As said by an American court on treason, "We cannot believe . . . that if a son was born in England to a foreign merchant, such son, on being afterwards taken in arms . . . should have [by England] been hung, drawn and quartered as a traitor." Or as said by John Locke, "And whoever was judged as a traitor or deserter, if he left or warred against a country, for being barely born in it of parents that were aliens there?" Hamdi precisely fits that bill, as said by our court and Locke. Hamdi was born here, but to parents temporarily present on business and who then returned to Saudi Arabia where Hamdi was raised.[2]

From a different perspective, not of the duties of the citizen to the nation but of the nation to the citizen, Hamdi's "presumed" citizenship does not look right either. Citizenship once held is zealously protected; government cannot pressure a citizen into relinquishing it. But it seems to have done so in the case of Hamdi. Reportedly, the United States dropped its charges against him in return for him agreeing to leave the country and to renounce whatever claim he had to citizenship. But citizenship, if genuine, ought not to be a chip in plea bargaining, should not be subject to forfeiture under

---

1. Tomoya Kawakita v. United States, 343 U.S. 717 (1952). President Eisenhower later commuted the death sentence to life imprisonment at Alcatraz. In 1963 Kawakita was pardoned by President Kennedy. *See also* Harisiades v. Shaughnessy, 342 U.S. 580, 585–86 (1950) ("The alien retains immunities from burdens which the citizen must shoulder").

2. Ludlam v. Ludlam, 26 N.Y. 356 (1963). The seriousness and severity of treason is shown by Michael Walzer, in his book *Obligations* (1982), as follows: "We have a number of words in the English language that describe the act of breaking faith with our fellow men: treason, treachery, betrayal. But we have only one word, or one in common use, that describes the man who breaks faith: we call him a traitor." Was Hamdi so related to us as to have "broken faith"? Surely not.

duress. Instead, any repudiation of it must be wholly volitional, and from all that appears that was not the case with Hamdi.[3] Instead, whatever he had he gave up under pressure of being tried again if he did not renounce his citizenship. On the whole, the point out of Hamdi's case is simply this: today and as push may come to shove, as it did in Hamdi's case, birthright citizenship is a matter of some confusion. In the next several paragraphs I detail some matters that hopefully are useful in dispelling the confusion.

In 1787 our Constitution referred to and spoke of the citizen but did not define the term. In time, though, these omissions proved costly and then they were addressed. After the Civil War and in expiation of a wrong — the exclusion of African Americans from citizenship — definition and identification of the citizen was necessary. In 1868 that was done by the Fourteenth Amendment. The first sentence of the Amendment states, "All persons born . . . in the United States, and subject to the jurisdiction thereof, are citizens of the United States and of the state wherein they reside."

The first part of that sentence, of dropping racism, was done by its opening statement of "All persons." Before the Amendment African Americans were not citizens. That they were not was as much as anything owed to the Supreme Court's decision in *Dred Scott*, 60 U.S. 393 (1857). By decision, and otherwise by considerable bad practice, they could not be citizens. The Fourteenth Amendment had to make African Americans citizens, and it did so, for them and all of us, with the Amendment's "All persons" opening. Here, in short form, is how.

---

3. As expressed in Afroyim v. Rusk, 387 U.S. 253 (1967), "To enforce expatriation or exile against a citizen without his consent is not a power anywhere belonging to this Government." More fully stated, the Court's position was that:

[W]e reject the idea . . . that . . . Congress has any general power, express or implied, to take away an American citizen's citizenship without his assent. This power cannot . . . be sustained as an implied attribute of sovereignty possessed by all nations. Other nations are governed by their own constitutions, if any, and we can draw no support from theirs. In our country the people are sovereign and the Government cannot sever its relationship to the people by taking away their citizenship. . . . (I)t belongs and appertains to the citizen and not to the Government. . . .

*See also* Perkins v. Elg, 307 U.S. 325 (1939); Norio Kiyama v. Rusk, 291 F.2d 10 (9th Cir. 1961); McGrath v. Tadayasu Abo, 186 F.2d 766 (9th Cir. 1951). To be sure, certain acts can cost a person his citizenship, at 8 U.S.C. § 1481. But the nearest of those acts to Hamdi, "entering, or serving in, the armed forces of a foreign state if . . . such armed forces are engaged in hostilities against the United States," was in dispute in his case. He claimed he had not been serving with the Taliban.

As said, in 1787 our Constitution defined neither the citizen nor how to be one. But in the next several years the practice that developed was that a person born to a citizen was by that birth, birth to a citizen, also a citizen. That practice, though, did not apply to African Americans. By no means could African Americans be citizens nor could their children. The problem then, after the Civil War, was how to bring them into citizenship. The measure we adopted, by the Fourteenth Amendment, was how to do so.

The measure the Amendment used came originally from Great Britain, where it was conceived in 1608 but for a different reason. In a famous decision in 1608, *Calvin's Case*, Britain departed from the practice that had prevailed in the kingdom, of subjectship gained by birth to a subject, from just that, birth to a subject. The new ruling, of *Calvin's Case,* was instead, place of birth alone subjectship. In 1603 England and Scotland had joined in a new British union. Queen Elizabeth had died without an immediate heir and the throne was empty. James VI, her cousin and king of Scotland, was invited to succeed her under a new title of James I. The new union, of Scotland and England, was legalized in *Calvin's Case*.

The party in the action, one Calvin had been born in Scotland before James had come into a new reign over both Scotland and England. But James had in the meantime become ruler of England as well as Scotland. In *Calvin's Case* one ruling might have been that as Calvin was born to parents who had been James' subjects in Scotland, by that measure, of Calvin being James' subject, he remained James' subject as James now ruled both Scotland and England. Yet, the land in question in *Calvin's Case* was in England and not Scotland. The court avoided that and other issues by its new ruling, that is, subjectship turned on only where a subject was born. Calvin was born in the reign of James IV, however that reign was established, and by that ruling the property Calvin that claimed was in the power of the British court.

Calvin's Case is a case of several significant parts, all significant to us. For the introduction we speak of the case only as the forerunner to birthright citizenship to the Fourteenth Amendment.

"All persons born in the United States" was the first part of the Citizenship Clause. The second part was "subject to the jurisdiction." As soon as an unqualified place of birth and nothing else was offered in the Senate, it caused a consternation reported by the Congressional Globe as an "undertone." Immediately, Sen. William Pitt Fessenden, a republican of Maine and a capable leader in the cause for civil rights, stood to object to the unadorned proposal of birth and that alone. His objection was by an example, by Fessenden saying, "Suppose a person is born here of parents from abroad temporarily in this country?" (As in the modern case of Yasser Haman Hamdi you might say.) "Temporarily in this country" was but one of a number of concerns owed to the fact that place of birth was by itself not an assurance of a good affiliation with the United States. Fessenden's question was a point of departure toward gaining the assurance.

After Fessenden's question, the Senate republicans went into a four-day caucus, and came out with the first sentence of the Amendment in its present form, "All persons born . . . in the United States, and subject to the jurisdiction thereof, are citizens of the United States."[4] "All persons born in the United States" was inclusive of African Americans and "subject to the jurisdiction" required of all a genuine connection to the United States.

A "genuine connection" to the United States must include the parents. Social facts in a family mean that the parents' feelings about the nation are transferred to their children. Consequently, parents who are US citizens do transfer those feelings to the child. Thus, that child gains birthright citizenship and the genuine connection is maintained. Yet, genuine connection also counts where the parents are *not* citizens. As noncitizen parents have lawfully settled among us on a permanent basis, as legal permanent residents and as such have assumed duties of loyalty, taxes, and military service expected of citizens, these immigrants should be fairly provided entitlements, which include birthright citizenship — as was held to be so, in cases entered not long after the enactment of the Fourteenth Amendment, for Scottish immigrants by the highest court of New Jersey in *Benny v. O'Brien* and for Chinese immigrants by the US Supreme Court in *United States v. Wong Kim*. In both the cases immigrant parents were not yet citizens. But in both cases the parents were here for the long run and were lawfully and permanently settled and living responsively and responsibly in the manner of citizens. Accordingly, the courts found that their children were entitled to birthright citizenship under the Fourteenth Amendment.

So far I have sketched in how it is and why it is the Citizenship Clause of the Fourteenth Amendment sets two conditions for birthright citizenship: birth on US soil and "subject to the jurisdiction." Today, probably the salient fact about the Clause is that the only remembered part of it is the place of birth. For instance, over the years the media has spoken of

---

4. Fessenden's question is at Cong. Globe, 39th Cong., 1st Sess. at 2768–69, 2869. The simple place of birth proposal, which had been offered by Senator Webb of Ohio, was thereafter withdrawn in favor of the proposal that became the present Citizenship Clause. The entire sequence of events is discussed in Chapter 5 on the Fourteenth Amendment.

"maternity tourism." At its high end this business consists of travel pack-
ages going for $60,000 or includes a few weeks at a spa or such in the United
States and then medical accommodations, so that at the end of the stay a
child is born here. The child, it is said, is born as a citizen and the mother
and child go back to parents' home country. The whole business turns on
the thought that US citizenship is, for the child, thus gained.[5] The activity
is presented as a despicable but yet unavoidable outcome of the constitutional standard for birthright citizenship. At this point the media quotes
the "All persons born in the United States" condition of the Fourteenth
Amendment but overlooks the just as necessary "subject to the jurisdiction" condition. As "subject to the jurisdiction" is ignored, birthright citizenship for persons only "temporarily present" is allowed. The point I wish
to now make, though, or rather introduce, is this: Why is it that the requirement of connection, as set by "subject to the jurisdiction," is so much
ignored?

The obvious reason is today's large presence, of eleven million or more,
of illegal immigrants in our country. Strong interests and opinions have
formed around them, for reasons that in part sound in politics and money.
For them birthright citizenship stands to validate their presence in the
United States. Accordingly, anything that ups the ante for that citizenship,
past place of birth as "subject to the jurisdiction" does, stands to be opposed.
An instance is provided in 1995 congressional hearings on birthright citizenship for illegal aliens. In those hearings the idea of permanent legal residency by illegal immigrants was denied, as "temporary visitors" were thought
to be ineligible for such citizenship. The testimony, by Professor Neuman
of Columbia Law School, was that "Nothing in the language of the Citizenship Clause, its legislative history, or its traditional interpretation,
requires that the parents of a child born in the United States must be permanent residents, rather than temporary visitors." (Then what was Senator
Fessenden's point, against the proposal that birthright citizenship requires
only place of birth, in asking about parents "temporarily in this country"?)
The point of Professor Neuman's testimony was that the only thing that
counts for birthright citizenship for illegal aliens is their presence on US
soil. Just and only that. The apparent intend of the testimony effect was to

---

5. The less expensive end of the business, crossing the border either illegally or on
a legal short-term basis and on this side having a baby delivered, perhaps at public
expense, operates differently but is directed to the same expected result, birthright
citizenship. Societal and Legal Issue Surrounding Children Born in the United States
to Illegal Alien Parents, Subcommittee on the Constitution, House Judiciary Committee, 105th Cong. 1st Sess. (1995).

terminate "subject to the jurisdiction" part of the Amendment.[6] But the intent has not worked, as in time we will see.

The following chapters include a historical narrative, commencing with the identification of "living well" as first spoken of by Aristotle, "living well" being the realization of a human capacity for living by and within a citizenry. Thereafter, I identify our conception of that capacity, starting at Plymouth and Jamestown. Then on out, the book is about the citizen, how we conceived the word in 1776, and then used it in the original Constitution and the Fourteenth Amendment. The final two chapters are about an impact, a moral impact, of unlawful immigration on the citizen.

---

6. Remarks of Professor Neuman in the 1995 hearings on Societal and Legal Issue Surrounding Children Born in the United States to Illegal Alien Parents, Subcommittee on the Constitution, House Judiciary Committee, 105th Cong. 1st Sess. 10 (1995). Professor Neuman was addressing and denying the conclusion of Professors Peter Schuck and Rogers Smith, in *Citizenship Without Consent* (1985), that legal permanent residency as claimed by illegal immigrants is a basis for birthright citizenship. From all is known by their undocumented status, they are not necessarily here on an enduring basis. Regarding "subject to the jurisdiction," Professor Neuman well aware of the "subject to the jurisdiction" requirement offered a view, of some sort of "partial jurisdiction," which annulled "subject to the jurisdiction." "Partial jurisdiction" is examined in Chapter 5 on the Fourteenth Amendment.

# Chapter Two

# Democracy Turns Up in North America

When English settlers first came to North America, republic government on the side of the Atlantic the settlers had departed had gone by the boards.[7] England and Europe were ruled by hereditary monarchs and people were subjects. They had no power, were suppressed within a class-dominated society, and were told it was God's plan. Still, amidst the kingdoms and fealties of England and Europe not a fact but a memory of persons quite different than subjects had survived. It persisted in history, where Athens, Rome, and some city states of northern Italy were remembered and where there had been persons who are today called citizens. It had been nourished by the recovery of classic work from Greece and Rome lost amidst the Dark Ages in which the citizen is identified. Accounts of that survival, of the classical idea of the citizen, can be found in Paul Magnette's *Citizenship: The History of an Idea*; Philip Brook Manville's *The Origins of Citizenship in Ancient Athens*; Peter Riesenberg's *Citizenship in the Western Tradition: Plato to Rousseau*, and on the point of civic humanism among city states of Northern Europe, in J. G. A Pocock's *The Machiavellian Moment*.

Although the idea of the citizen survived, for us that survival can in a way be overstated, as we may think that the citizenry that arose on this side of the Atlantic sprouted from seeds out of Athens. But this was not the case; instead, our first moments of citizens and self-government — the impulses

---

7. North America was then inhabited by several million people, the Native Americans who had come here from Eastern Asia and perhaps stone-age Europe. These peoples lived together in social and political arrangements that were tribal. Those arrangements, though, seemed to have no impact on the civic arrangements of the seventeenth-century arrivals from Europe.

that then carried down to the Revolution — were of our own making. When in 1620 the religious separatists at Plymouth established self-government dedicated to the common good, they did so out of their own idea — not of a classical but as much as anything of a religious origin — of a covenant among them freely arrived at and directed toward the common good. When in 1618 self-government came to Jamestown, it proceeded not from classical learning but from a hard-nosed, proprietary decision by directors of the Virginia Company, about gaining settlers and a settlement fit enough to make a go of it in the hard times of North America. I will shortly cover these seminal instances of democracy in America. For the moment, the single point is: While a republic, or a democracy as I should say, as begun in America can be understood by reference by classical learning that learning did not cause the commencement. Rather, we came into it our own way.

However, I do not otherwise mean to dismiss the classical idea of democracy; its worth remains considerable. In part, the value sounds in language. We are a species that lives within a grammar. Without words for the form of a thing it may not be perceived well. For democracy, the ancient Greeks established the terms. They created the word, *demokratis, demos* being people, *kratis* being force, and thus power to the people. This power enabled a measure of a good life that translates as "living well." When at Athens they spoke of living well, they knew it required a dedicated space and identified that space as the *polis*. Athens further understood that living well within that space required human actors of a particular sort and identified them as *polites,* to us "citizens." The essential *polis–polites* relation was itself named *politeia,* meaning for us today a citizenry. Within the grammar thus constructed, the assertion made in the introduction to this book — that should the citizenry disintegrate, the nation will not necessarily die but it will no longer be democratic — is clear and sensible.

Although the terms established at Athens are important, more important is the idea — the classic idea of the citizen — encompassed by these terms. Those terms wrapped around a spirit that consists of the better parts of human nature. Perhaps, I might introduce these parts by reference to a predicament, a modern social problem really, first stated by Jean-Jacques Rousseau. As said by Rousseau, "If it was a matter of hunting deer everyone well realized that he must remain faithfully at his post; but if a hare happened to pass within reach of one of them, we cannot doubt that he would have gone off in pursuit of it." So, what is to keep that man from chasing rabbits? You might answer, "Enlightened self-interest" (the hunter and his family stand to lose a share of the larger game of present and future hunts), and there is considerable sense to this answer. Still, enlightened or not, self-interest will not necessarily keep that hunter at his post. Something else is necessary, which is trust.

# At Athens: Living Well

The *polis*, Aristotle said, "exists not only for the sake of living but rather primarily for the sake of living well." Interestingly, the Greeks had a word for those who did not understand this. The word that we will immediately recognize, but the original context probably not. The word is idiot—in Greek, *idiotes*. Today, we may romanticize the loner, the lone wolf who stands on his own outside the community. We do so notwithstanding the fact that in nature that animal is usually so weakened as not to be fit for much. Hardheaded as they were, the Greeks had no illusions about such beings. To Aristotle, the person "who by nature and not by mere accident" was aloft of community was "a bad man" and useless as such, like "an isolated piece" in chess. Pericles had earlier made that same point, saying that, "It is only we who regard the one, not participating in these duties, not as unambitious but as useless." And their word for that person was *idiotes*.

From a viewpoint of enlightened self-interest, we can readily see that a capacity for communal living underwrites our success as species on the planet. Efficiently, we watch each other's backs, and share and divide labor. Living well, though, included more than that. It is not a simple matter of material well-being. That much could be expected of animals, and in fact Aristotle spoke of those who had no greater end than material well-being in mind as mere animals. He ascribed a higher goal to those whom he referred to as *zoon politikon*, which translates as political animals. He spoke of them as *naturally* virtuous and civically inclined beings and as such part of and essential to living well. These beings, the citizens actually, he said, are a "creation of nature." Aristotle thus posited a couple of things: one being that the citizen is driven by a moral force that is naturally infused, as by evolution or as "written on the heart" as expressed by the Apostle Paul and by Greek and Roman Stoics. The other is that this force by its own motion produces a palpable happiness. Virtue is its own reward, as we say. Or as more completely stated by Edmund Spenser, apparently by reading Aristotle, in *The Faerie Queene*: "Your vertue selfe her owne reward shall breed, Euen immortall praise, and glory wyde." This part of virtue, the self and public respect it included, was much in the Greek mind. Pericles, in his funerary oration for warriors fallen in battle, spoke of "the noblest of sepulchers . . . the memory of the Athenian people."

Virtue as essential to living well was described as *arête*, which seems at once the goodness, force, and purpose of a citizen. Originally, as by Homer, *arête* was an excellence in design and function, as a well-tuned violin or a well-sharpened knife and valued as such. As *arête*—now an excellence in civic living—is a matter of design and function and as such (according to modern studies) an outcome of evolution, for humankind evolution has not so much produced a disposition to tooth and claw as it has a certain selflessness: A disposition to give of oneself, dramatically as with the fallen warrior and prosaically, but as essentially, in the day-to-day life of the *polis*.

Aristotle defined the citizen in terms of action, saying that a citizen did not become that by occupying space: "Nor is a citizen a citizen through residing in a place." Instead, action in that space in the manner of a citizen was necessary. Accordingly, Athenians paid jurors a small amount, so that persons too poor to give up that time could do so, and thus be better realized as citizens. For our own democracy, Thomas Jefferson addressed that realization, as he wrote, "Where every man is a sharer in the direction of his ward-republic, or of some of the higher ones, and feels that he is a participator in the government of affairs, not merely at an election one day in the year, but every day; ... he will let the heart be torn out of his body sooner than his power be wrested from him by a Caesar or a Bonaparte." Brian O'Connell in *Civil Society: The Underpinnings of American Democracy*, quietly makes the same point, saying, "As we experience the benefits of so much citizen participation, including the personal satisfactions that such involvement provides, we became all the more committed to this kind of participatory society. Along the way, we constantly renewed our faith in the basic intelligence and ability of people." Or as succinctly stated by Paul Magnette, "Citizenship is only itself when activity is added to status."[8]

As Aristotle spoke of the traits of a citizen, he understood that not all persons hold these traits, or hold them to varying degrees, and that those holding these traits might lose them. These understandings led to two conclusions, the first one being that democracy is not necessarily the right choice for all people everywhere. That democracy is not the best choice for all people turns on a close examination of all the circumstances of a people. In this respect, the method of the *Politics* is dialectic. Aristotle examined various forms of government (most prominently the various city states among which Athens was sited), so that viewing the "problems on both sides," a people might better determine "what is true and what is false." Or as Aristotle otherwise stated, "Where knowledge and philosophical wisdom are concerned, the ability to discern and hold in view the consequences of either hypothesis is no insignificant tool, since then it only remains to make a correct choice of one of them."

---

8. Writings of Thomas Jefferson to Joseph C Cabell (14:421–23), Letter 2 Feb. 1816, available at http://press-pubs.uchicago.edu/founders/documents/v1ch4s34.html; Brian O'Connell, *Civil Society: The Underpinnings of American Democracy*, 29 (1999); Paul Magnette, *Citizenship: The History of an Idea 15* (2005).

The second conclusion was that *if* citizenship is right for a people, they still had to work to sustain it. Although understanding that some better parts of human nature gave rise to citizenship, Aristotle understood that these parts might fail and with them the citizenry. Accordingly, the Athenians worked at maintaining citizenship, as by education, music, military training, civic ceremonies, theatre, and a respect for their gods. They saw civic participation as essential to civic minds; accordingly, they used public funds to underwrite participation in civic life. And otherwise they elevated the service and role of citizens, as by "the memory of the Athenian people."

For the record, the following are a few remarks about the *polis* and its members. The Greek *polis* was a civic body of a particular type, a "multitude of citizens." In structure, it included a legislative assembly, the *ecclesia*, and a judicial system. The assembly included the entire citizenry (all the *polites*) and it determined public measures by a vote of that whole. Within the assembly, all alike were *ho boulomenos* (he who wishes): each might be vibrant, and might stand to speak and initiate public measures and to oppose actions not to his liking. The judicial system consisted of courts composed of jurors, with each citizen being eligible to be and expected to act as a juror when called. A panel of 6,000 jurors was drawn each year; several hundred served each day. They heard cases of a smaller or private kind known as *dike* and of a larger or more public kind known as *graphe*, with a larger number of jurors assigned the latter cases.

The Greeks further identified the power of the citizen and denoted that power as *exousi*. It was held in equal measure by all who were citizens, and was not differentiated according to social, familial, or economic rank. Solon, in particular, had done away with hereditary aristocracy, so that a merchant, warrior, or artisan had the same power as the wealthy landowners who had comprised that aristocracy. Moreover, at times the *polis* acted positively, better to assure that in practice *exousi* was equal. For instance and as said, on understanding that poorer citizens could ill afford to serve as jurors, jurors were paid so they could act as citizens. But while internally—within the body of *polites*—citizenship was egalitarian, externally it was not. It was not open to women or to slaves. As I will later discuss, within the United States we in time differently and particularly deployed the egalitarian substance of citizenship, using it as a means, provided by the Fourteenth Amendment, of eradicating the ill effects of slavery.

A final and particular consideration, given the subject matter of this book, is: Exactly how was citizenship gained at Athens? It was gained as a right of birth. But of course, not everyone born anywhere gained Athenian citizenship, so what quality of birth gave rise to Athenian citizenship? Was it place of birth, as on Athenian soil? It was not. The Greeks located Athens spiritually as well as spatially; they referred to Athens as *hoi Athenaoi*, meaning the body of citizens. (Or as it has been said by the Supreme Court bench, "This Nation's citizenry is the country and the country is its citizenry."[9]) Accordingly, at Athens birthright citizen was determined not by a geographic place of birth but by birth to citizens; it was, as Plato said, a matter of "descent from citizen parents."

Philip Brook Manville opens his book, *The Origins of Citizenship in Ancient Athens*, with an account of birthright citizenship at Athens, as follows: "The scene is an Athenian court, about 345 BC. The speaker is expressing his outrage that a foreign prostitute and her Athenian 'husband,' through their wanton behavior and illegal registration of children have disgraced the laws of Athenian citizenship, something 'worthy and sacred'." As then noted by Manville, at Athens, "aliens who illegally adopted the status" were punished.[10]

## The *Res Publica* and the Civic Humanists

At Rome as at Athens, citizens for a time gathered in service of the common good. The form established at Athens was followed. At Rome the space essential to that service was denoted as *res publica*, then literally the thing of the people, and today and to us the republic. *Civi* denoted, in particular, the citizen within the space, and *civitas* the citizen–state relationship.

In practice, the citizen was not as fully realized in Rome as at Athens. The final extent of Roman territory, from the British Isles to the near east and across North African, seems part of the reason. Unless accounted for (as by federalism in our Constitution), this breadth of places and peoples stood to limit citizenship, certainly citizenship as active self-rule. Still, the 450 years of the Roman Republic, from about 500 BCE to the rise of the Empire at 50 BCE, included a measure of citizenship. Persons thus engaged were known as *cives Romani*. But as the republic expanded, taking in new territories, a differentiated sort of citizenship became the norm, as in *sine suffragio*, that is, citizenship without political engagement. Eventually, *civitas* was diluted to the point of extinction. In AD 212, the Emperor Caracalla proclaimed that everyone in the empire was a citizen. Apparently, he did so to increase the tax base. The only Roman historian to speak of this matter

---

9. Afroyim v. Rusk, 387 U.S. 253, 268 (1967).

10. Philip B. Mannville, *The Origins of Citizenship in Ancient Athens* 3–4 & n.3 (1990).

wrote, "This was the reason why he made all the people in his empire Roman citizens; nominally he was honoring them, but his real purpose was to increase his revenues."[11] The numbers, rather than the stature of citizens, had been increased; the people the emperor declared to be *civis* were by no means engaged as such. They were nationals (*Romanus*) but were short of being citizens, and *civitas* disappeared.

Here is a description of that which had disappeared. Citizenship at Athens and Rome had been appreciated by the philosophical school of Stoics and particularly in the works of Cicero. About the citizen, as understood by the Stoics, here is a paragraph taken from a piece by Anthony Long on *Stoic Communitarianism and Normative Citizenship*:

> Stoicism is the ancient philosophy most relevant to modern politics and civic education. Its relevance is due ... to its theory that the human good depends primarily on rationality and excellence of character. ... Reflection on the norms of human nature persuaded the Stoics that we all share a common interest in living just and mutually beneficial lives. This principle ... makes rationality and integrity, rather than material prosperity, the essential values of community and the measure of normative citizenship and lawmaking.[12]

The Edict of Caracalla being a sign of the fact, citizenship disappeared from Europe until the late Middle Ages, when events created spaces where it might come back and for a time it did. In AD 1183, the Peace of Constance — at the hands of the Holy Roman Emperor Frederick Barbarossa — provided a measure of independence to cities in northern Italy. Within that independence and for these cities, commercial, civic, and artistic life was enriched. Consequently, those cities needed to gain and retain artisans, physicians, and merchants. A concept of civic life, in which government is the enterprise of its people, was seen as a means to that end. And at that time, classic writing and the idea of the citizen also resurfaced. Marsilius of Padua, a scholar much taken with the Italian city states, proclaimed that, "A citizen I define in accordance with Aristotle." In a significant movement, among those city states that is today known as "civic humanism," that definition was realized.

As with Aristotle, people in these city states did not become a citizen by inhabiting a place. Rather, and as is usefully described by Paul Magnette, one became a citizen by living according to "a gathering of people formed

---

11. Cassius Dio, *Roman History*, Book 78, Ch. 9.

12. Anthony A. Long, Stoic Communitarianism and Normative Citizenship, 24 *Soc. Philos. Policy* 241–61 (2007).

to live justly." As more fully stated by Magnette, "Thus they are not called citizens of the same commune because they were accepted together inside the same walls, but rather citizens are those who have agreed to live justly under one law." Although these city states banked on a rational morality, on that spark that caused humans cohesively and coherently to care and act for each other, they also understood that the spark might be quenched. Consequently, they sought to sustain it as best they could. Three helping ways were then (concisely) identified by the Florentine chancellor and historian, Leonardi Bruni, as follows: "The hope of attaining honor and raising oneself up is equal for everyone." Internally, "honor" is a sense of integrity and thus of self-confidence and self-worth; externally it is a recognition by the community that reinforces the individual. "Raising oneself up" includes the chance to better oneself. Honor and raising oneself up were modified by "equal." Equal, as in having the same chance as anyone, is valued by worthy people; thus, by offering equality, the city might better attract and hold people.

Also examined in those city states was: How does one become a citizen? Birthright citizenship was the main way, as gained at Athens and Rome by descent from citizen parents. As well and toward the end of gaining people of needed skill sets, processes we would identify as naturalization were in place in those states.

## Plymouth and Hobbes

Understanding — that the virtue that at once enables and is a consequence of democracy — is innate, yet leaves one knowing that that quality is not uniformly distributed within the species. Individuals are worthy in greater or lesser respects. Still, virtuous persons can be found and aggregated in an amount sufficient to constitute a citizenry. Were this not so, the venture that began on our northern shores, at Plymouth in 1620, would have failed. Before the winds, the ninety men, women, and children aboard the Mayflower and en route to the "northern parts of Virginia" had been driven pretty far north, to colder, rockier shores and thinner soil and hardships and dangers they could not fully know. But they had some idea, as recorded in William Bradford's journal; the day the Pilgrim's went ashore, they "were ready to perish in this wilderness." But they did not intend to: They gathered themselves and by the Mayflower Compact, they did "covenant and combine ourselves together into a Civil Body Politick." The end of this "Civil Body Politick" was "the General good," with that good determined by the settlers themselves. Otherwise stated, the Pilgrims reconstituted themselves as citizens rather than subjects.

To all ideas of the citizen and living well and covenants toward those ends, Thomas Hobbes (1588–1679), author of *The Leviathan* and the most prominent political philosopher of his time, said rubbish. Hobbes spoke of his work as scientific, as inductive and open-minded, viewing first the evidence and then drawing conclusions. In his words, "I ground the Civill Right of Soveraigns, and both the Duty and Liberty of Subjects, upon the known naturall inclinations of Mankind." Others had different views about his claim to science. Nonetheless, Hobbes dismissed Aristotle and similarly persuaded classicists as less than scientific, actually as nothing more than scribes proceeding by rote. As said by Hobbes, "[I]n these western parts of the world, we are made to receive our opinions concerning the Institutions and Rights of Common-wealths, from Aristotle, Cicero and other men, Greeks and Romanes, that lived under Popular States, derived those rights not from the Principles of Nature, but transcribed into their books, out of the practice of their own Common-wealths which were popular; as the Grammerians describe the Rules of Language."

That statement, though, seems an undue slight, considering that Aristotle referenced the "known naturall inclinations of Mankind" more comprehensively than did Hobbes and more thoroughly tested those inclinations by his dialectics. Accordingly, another Englishmen, Algernon Sydney, in roughly the same period as Hobbes, spoke for Aristotle's objectivity, saying, "Aristotle was not simply for Monarchy or against Popular Government; but approved or disapproved of either according to circumstances."

Citizenship entails a measure of selflessness and classicists viewed humankind as possessed of this measure to some greater or lesser extent. To Hobbes, this extent was lesser to the point of extinction. To him, rather than selfless, humankind is naturally and overwhelmingly self-absorbed, short-sighted, and selfish. As he looked into human nature, Hobbes did not see the citizen-enabling virtues viewed by the classicists. Instead he saw a beast, as in the aphorism he dusted off that "man is a wolf to man." With egoism thus taken as the human condition, life on this earth, if we were left to ourselves, would in Hobbes' famous but abysmal state of nature be "solitary, nasty, brutish, and short."

Hobbes thus made the case for sovereignty, for a lawmaker and a protection of law that stands against the predatory acts of humans on humans, the "warre of every man against every man." If this, preferring sovereignty over anarchy, were all Hobbes was about, his case is not one that anyone short of an anarchist disagrees with. But Hobbes went further: The sovereign he posited, *The Leviathan,* was of a particular form — that of the autocratic state, presumably the English royalty, where the people were subjects rather than citizens, where they were ruled rather than ruling, and where they lived in submission and in "dreade" of the king. Dread and superstition were especially important. As declared by Hobbes, "Justice, Equity, Modesty, Mercy . . . without the terrour or some power, to cause them to be observed are contrary to our natural passions."

There was "no peace without subjection." Hobbes feared liberty. He thought it begat licentiousness. Indeed, he disliked Aristotle and the classicists because their view of humanity shored up liberty and caused people to "hate Monarchy." "[I]t is an easy thing," he wrote, "for men to be deceived, by the specious name of Libertie." And "by reading of these Greeks, and Latine Authors, men from their childhood have gotten a habit (under a false show of Libertie) of favouring tumults, and of licentious controlling."

In his own time, Hobbes was doubted and doubted in terms of the very currency — the material of inductive reasoning — with which he said he worked. The Earl of Clarendon, in his work, *A Survey of Mr. Hobbes His Leviathan* (1696), questioned the evidence, asking, from what data did Hobbes glean his conclusions about human nature? Clarendon's answer? That that data was limited to introspection: "Mr. Hobbes having taken upon him to imitate God, and created Man after his own likeness, given him all the passions and affections which he finds himself." Hobbes himself lent some support to that judgement, in the form of sharp pieces of self-awareness. He spoke of himself as inclined to "commodious living" and of an "effeminate courage." He had lived comfortably within and been maintained by the English aristocracy, as a tutor and the like. Perhaps, he sensed that the life of a citizen included a hardness and risks to which he was not disposed.

Today, in light of different and more extensive study, as by modern biology and anthropology and by reference to different and larger data bases, Hobbes' assumption that "man is a wolf to man" seems a slight to wolves and more so to humankind. How this is so, how humans carry, unless we are so mindless as to extinguish it, the spark that enables citizens, I shall discuss in a later chapter. In the meantime, on this side of Atlantic, Hobbes' assumptions about the capacities of humankind were disproved as he wrote them.

# At Plymouth

In 1620 and at Plymouth, the settlers had sailed beyond the reach of the Leviathan. Owing to what the English Crown would later refer to as "the remote distances of those places," these settlers were effectively outside the power and protection of the monarchy. But the Pilgrims were not therefore at a loss. Instead and as said by the Mayflower Compact, they did "covenant and combine ourselves together into a civil Body Politick," the end of which was "the General good" as they themselves would determine and enforce.

Covenant is an interesting word and an elevated concept. In biblical origin, it means binding a people by word, with that connection marked by ceremony and oath. Our Constitution is of that order; its first words are "We the people" and the commitments then made were sealed by special assemblies within the states. Of this whole notion of covenants dependent on the commitment of a people, Hobbes was particularly contemptuous. They might be possible among insects, he wrote, but not among human beings. "The agreement of creatures [ants and bees]," he wrote, "is Natural; that of men is by Covenant only, which is Artificial." Artificial and unworkable for human beings, Hobbes thought, because of their egoism; consequently, it was of "no wonder if there be somewhat else required (besides Covenant) to make their Agreement constant and lasting."[13] For Hobbes, the essential "something else" was a king, "A power to keep them in awe" and to attend "as he shall think expedient, for their Peace and Common Defense."

No matter, the Pilgrims did as Hobbes said they could not. By covenant they formed "a Civil Body Politick" and determined that apart from their "Dreade King James" they would provide for and enforce "such just and equal Laws" as fitted the "General good of the Colony."[14] Thereafter, this

---

13. Perhaps Hobbes wrote against the "Agreement of the People," by which (amidst English Civil War) the Levelers (described in the Prologue) had tried to supplant royalty with a commonwealth. As to bees and ants today we agree with Hobbes that their cooperation is natural and attribute it to kinship, to their close genetic connection. We disagree that covenants among human beings are impossible, *see, e.g.,* the United States Constitution.

14. Here is the Compact, exactly as recorded by William Bradford in the *History of Plymouth Plantation*:

In yᵉ name of God Amen· We whose names are underwriten, the loyall subjects of our dread soveraigne Lord King James by yᵉ grace of God, of great Britaine, Franc, & Ireland king, defender of yᵉ faith, &c. Haveing undertaken, for yᵉ glorie of God, and advancemente of yᵉ Christian faith and honour of our king & countrie, a voyage to plant yᵉ first colonie in yᵉ Northerne parts of Virginia, doe by these presents solemnly & mutualy in yᵉ presence of God, and one of another, covenant & combine our selves togeather into a civill body politick; for our better ordering, & preservation & furtherance of yᵉ ends aforesaid; and by vertue

kind of agreement iterated throughout the northern colonies, as in the Providence Agreement of 1637, where the settlers did "promise to subject ourselves in active and passive obedience to all such orders or agreements as shall be made for the public good of the body in an orderly way." They agreed to submit to "orders . . . for the public good." Orders as made by whom? By themselves, through self-government according to, as they said, "the major consent of present inhabitants."

In these agreements, as the colonists established self-government, initial references as in the Mayflower Compact to the "dreade King" went by the boards.

Democracy as thus begun in New England began simple, small, and direct in town-hall meetings. And began amidst hardship unimagined in England but as to which in New England the advice given, for instance by John Winthrop, was essentially to man up. Winthrop's advice was: "No place of itself has afforded sufficient to the first inhabitants. Such things as we stand in need of are usually supplied by God's blessing upon the wisdom and industry of Man, and whatsoever we stand in need of is treasured up in the earth by the Creator to be fetched thence by the sweat of our brows. . . . We must learn with Paul to want as well as to abound. If we have food and raiment (which are there to be had) we ought to be contented. The difference in the quality may a little displease us, but it cannot hurt us."

A picture of civic government in those hard times is provided by a 1633 agreement at Dorchester, that "for the generall good and well ordering of the affayres of the Plantation their shall be every Mooneday before the Court by eight of the Clocke in the morning, and presently upon the beating of the drum, a generall meeting of the inhabitants of the Plantation att the meeteing house, there to settle (and sett downe) such orders as may tend to the general good as aforesaid." In time and in part for convenience, direct democracy of this sort evolved toward representative democracy, as by the Cambridge Agreement of 1634 that provided that seven persons should be chosen by the community at large and that "by a Joynt Consent that whatsoever these Townsmen thus Chosse shall doe in the

---

hearof, to enacte, constitute, and frame shuch just & equall lawes, ordinances, acts, constitutions, & offices, from time to time, as shall be thought most meete & convenient for y$^e$ generall good of y$^e$ Colonie: unto which we promise all due submission and obedience. In witnes wherof we have hereunder subscribed our names at Cap-Codd y$^e$ .11. of November, in y$^e$ year of raigne of our soveraigne lord King James of England, France, & Ireland y$^e$ eighteenth and of Scotland y$^e$ fiftie fourth. An$^o$: Dom. 1620.

Compas of ther tyme shall stand in full force as if the whole Town did the same."

The Fundamental Orders of Connecticut, entered into 1638 among settlers along the Connecticut River, was the first compact extensive enough to be referred to as a constitution. It differentiated and provided for legislative, executive, and judicial powers, and directed those powers to the common good. And referred to the polity thus created as a "Commonwealth." It also identified its citizens, them being "all that are admitted freemen and have taken the Oath of Fidelity, and do cohabit within this Jurisdiction." The citizen, or "freeman" as then said, was the person accepted by, living within, and of sworn allegiance to the polity. In origin, freeman had meant no longer being a serf. Now it also identified a person dedicated to the good of the whole community. By the oath known throughout New England as the Freemen's Oath, the person pledged that, "When I shall be called to give my voice touching any such matter of this State, in which Freemen are to deal, I will give my vote and suffrage as I shall judge in mine own conscience may best conduce and tend to the public weal of the body."[15]

A question that presents itself is: Where did the idea of democracy according to a covenant come from? Such covenants were not then the practice, not in England, Europe, or for that matter tribal government among

---

15. The oath was commonly required throughout New England. Its common form was that:

I _____being by Gods providence, an Inhabitant, and Freeman, within the Jurisdiction of this Commonwealth; do freely acknowledge myself to be subject to the Government thereof: And therefore do here swear by the great and dreadful Name of the Ever-living God, that I will be true and faithful to the same, and will accordingly yield assistance and support there unto, with my person and estate, as in equity I am bound; and will also truly endeavor to maintain and preserve all the liberties and privileges thereof, submitting myself to the wholesome Laws and Orders made and established by the same. And further, that I will not plot or practice any evil against it, or consent to any that shall so do; but will timely discover and reveal the same to lawful Authority now here established, for the speedy preventing thereof. Moreover, I do solemnly bind myself in the sight of God, that when I shall be called to give my voice touching any such matter of this State, in which Freemen are to deal, I will give my vote and suffrage as I shall judge in mine own conscience may best conduce and tend to the public weal of the body, So help me God in the Lord Jesus Christ.

Today and for Vermont, that oath is still required, by Section 42 of that state's constitution as follows: "You solemnly swear (or affirm) that whenever you give your vote or suffrage, touching any matter that concerns the State of Vermont, you will do it so as in your conscience you shall judge will most conduce to the best good of the same, as established by the Constitution, without fear or favor of any person."

Native Americans. A source of the idea, of democracy by covenant, has been simple common sense, the perception that the brutally hard times of the New World were best met by collective effort and intelligence and a pledge to work together. Another answer is that as much as anything, these covenants came out of Christianity and the capacities that religion recognizes in humans.

The parties to the Mayflower Compact were (in main part) Congregationalists. Rather than relying on a bishopric-directed faith (as in the Church of England), the Pilgrims believed that a congregation, itself and without clerical direction, best discerned the ways of God. Indeed, their movements prior the Plymouth, leaving England for the Netherlands and then departing the Netherlands for America, were determined communally and by compacts arrived at by common consent. In the New World, determinations were made and done in the same way, whether they pertained to the church or instead to civil government. Civil compacts thus spread and evolved throughout New England, among Puritans as well as Congregationalists. These compacts had a different take on civil government, turned on a different view of nature, than that of Hobbes and the royalists he supported. As these New Englanders saw it, human nature had been conceived by the mind of God and as conceived was of a different order than that posited by Hobbes. Accordingly, the Fundamental Orders of Connecticut provided that where "a people are gathered together the word of God requires that to maintain the peace and union of such a people there should be an orderly and decent Government." The "orderly and decent government" best for them was, as they said, a commonwealth, self-government directed to the common good. Reference to the Crown and its "dreade power" dropped out of their agreements.

In time, New England produced as full a description of the citizen and the "body politic" as we have today. In its preamble, the Massachusetts Constitution of 1780 asserted that, "The body politic is formed by a voluntary association of individuals, it is a social compact, by the whole people covenants with each citizen, and each citizen with the whole people, that all shall be government by certain laws for the common good."

# At Jamestown

The Mayflower Compact was in 1620. About a year earlier and at Jamestown, democracy had also come to North America, but now by a different route. The settlement at Jamestown was a proprietary venture of the London Company, an association of speculators of various assumptions (generally wrong) about profits to be gained from the New World. On May 14, 1607, after a long voyage of four months, three ships brought 105 settlers ashore, at a low, partly sandy, partly marshy strip of land, nearly surrounded by the James River and as such deemed more defensible. They called this place Jamestown and it became the first permanent English settlement in North America.

Unlike the middle-class settlers at Plymouth, the 105 settlers who came ashore at Jamestown were of varying abilities. Slightly more than half were listed as "gentlemen," which generally meant not used to working. The remainder was workingmen of various sorts, carpenter, bricklayers, twelve "laborers," four "boys," and a few of other backgrounds, which included a military professional, Captain John Smith. No farmers were among them. The returns the company expected were from activities such as gold mining, glass manufacture, and silk production, and locating a passage to China. (The London Company had instructed the settlers to seek a river that "bendeth most toward the Northwest," as they thought toward China.) In terms of government, Jamestown was under the strict control of the Company, by a council of five selected by the Company, and by a detailed set of orders that regulated daily life and labor in minute detail. In short, direction of the settlement was detailed, top-down, and from London.

Thus settled and organized, the settlers at Jamestown did not "live well" in the meaning of Aristotle or any meaning of the words. Within six months of their landing, 74 of 105 had died. Those deaths and many thereafter were described by one of the settlers, George Percy, as follows: "Our men were destroyed by cruel diseases such as swelling, Flixes, Burning Fevers, and by warres, and some departed suddenly, but for the most they died of meere famine." The "warres" were attacks by members of indigenous peoples, the Powhatans, who were alternately helpful as they provided food and local knowledge to Englishmen who knew nothing of the land and hurtful as they from time to time killed settlers. The Powhatans were under tribal government and a chief who both aided and used the English, used them as instruments of his own alliances and intrigues among the tribes. As related by Percy, the Native Americans were "nott soe simple."[16]

---

16. And were not to be treated as children: In speaking of the boneheaded supervision of Jamestown by Company directors, John Smith, in particular, objected to starting an arms race in the New World, saying, "their kind friends [the Powhatans] they trained up so well to shoot in a piece to hunt and kill them fowl." John Smith, *Advertisements for the Inexperienced Planters of New England, or Anywhere or the Pathway to Experience to Erect a Plantation*, Ch. I (1631).

From time to time, Jamestown was replenished with new settlers but they too perished in large numbers. The years 1609–1610 were known as the starving time and in these years about three-quarters of the settlers died. Why had things gone so badly? Captain John Smith, the veteran the London Company had appointed to the governing council, had assumed a leadership role in the settlement, had an answer. According to Smith, the problem was not "the barreness and defect of the Countrie" but instead a "want of providence, industrie and government." In time, these problems were addressed.

The London Company's notions about profitable enterprises, as by gold mining, glass manufacture, and silk production, had been wholly wrong. In time, John Rolfe, a competent gentlemen and otherwise remembered as Pocahontas' second husband, produced a profitable export, tobacco of a sweeter strain than the native plant, and brought an immediate success back to England. But more than a money crop was needed. The company suffered from a lack of competent people and on top of them bad government.

Competent meant people of practical skills. The first settlers at Jamestown had come from the ends, top and bottom, of English society. The top had supplied downwardly mobile aristocrats, second sons who under English law inherited no part of their parents' title or estate. As they sought to secure their fortunes at Jamestown, these lesser aristocrats simply lacked the ability. The bottom end of the order, the commoners at Jamestown, farmers and first-rate artisans were lacking. Among all the settlers, bad conduct as in thievery and hoarding was common.

As to government and as said, the colony at Jamestown was managed top-down from London, by Company directors of the "conceit" they could preside over the colony without on the ground experience. Of which John Smith provided a first-hand account: The settlers at Jamestown "were subject to some few here in London who were never there" and who "consumed all in arguments, projects, and their own conceits; every year trying new conclusions, altering everything yearly as they altered opinions, till they had consumed [over the first few years] more than £200,000 and near 8000 men's lives."[17] For these defects, respecting incompetent people and bad direction, the remedy, as prescribed in 1618, is of a particular interest.

Coordination of abilities and resources essential to survival in hard circumstances was lacking and it became apparent that the problem was a matter of governance. The colony was structured along corporate and

---

17. John Smith, *Advertisements for the Inexperienced Planters of New England, or Anywhere or the Pathway to Experience to Erect a Plantation*, Ch. I (1631).

communistic lines and as said managed top-down from London, which resulted in mismanagement. Perhaps not so evidently, the system was also demoralizing. Here is a description of the total result by an original settler, Ralph Hamor:

> [W]hen our people were fedde out of the common store and laboured jointly in the manuring of the ground, and planting corne, glad was that man that could slippe from his labour,. . . neither cared they for the increase, presuming that howsoeuer their harvest prospered, the generall store must maintain them, by which meanes we reaped not so much corne from the labours of 30 men, as three men haue done for themselues.[18]

Stated differently, within the settlement initially ordered at Jamestown shirking and free riding were prevalent.

But within the London Company things were changing. Sir Edwin Sandys, of a more liberal bent, had gained a leadership role and successfully backed some innovations. One of which was a move away from centralized control and toward a free market structure within the colony. The structure centered on private property and property rights and freely traded goods and the energy it all infused. Settlers who had arrived before 1616 gained 100 acres of land; new settlers who paid their own way to Jamestown received 50 acres for themselves and an additional 50 acres for each person they brought with them. As well, the acres thus gained were unencumbered by feudalistic tenures as in England. With settlers now owning the land they worked and its produce, output increased.

There was more, consisting of new measures meant to at once eliminate top-down control and attract better people to the settlement. *This measure was a move toward self-government*, the idea of which, as explained by Edwin Sandys, was that the settlers themselves might better "execute those things, as might best tend to their good" and that "every man will more willingly obey lawes to which he hath yielded his consent." Accordingly, the Company allowed for a "General Assembly" that included Burgesses elected for each town, plantation, or hundred (a hundred acre allotment). In short, the Company provided for governance by means of representatives elected from each community along the James River. That governance was directed to the common good. In furtherance of the "publiqe weale of the said colony," the General Assembly was to "enact such general lawes and orders for the behoof of the of the said colony and the good government thereof as

---

18. Ralph Hamor, *A True Discourse of the Present Estate of Virginia, and the Successes of the Affaires There till the 18 of Iune, 1614* (1615), available at http://memory.loc.gov

shall from time to tyme appear necessarie or requisite." Within the General Assembly, laws were made according to the majority vote of those present.

As established at Jamestown, democracy was at first neither complete nor entire. For instance, General Assembly enactments were subject to a veto by a company-appointed governor. But however much this was an initially modest serving of democracy it was still a portion that could not be withdrawn. From it, democracy evolved in various ways. By various measures and evasions, the colonists doggedly avoided the sting of executive vetoes, either by the Company or the Crown, of their actions through their General Assembly. Through it all, practical experience in translating the will of people into action was gained. Extensive local government, as by counties, was in time put in place. Practical skills, in matters of taxes and public budgets, developed. Assurance of unimpeded democratic processes through measures, such as an elected representative's immunity from arrest while about legislative work, came about. Over time a bicameral government and separation of powers developed. Out of Virginia and at the time of Constitution, we had eight generations of experience in democratic government and drew on it as the Constitution was drafted. We were not exactly novices.[19]

## Crèvecoeur's Pot

Michel Guillaume Jean de Crèvecoeur was a son of French aristocrats who made his way to the New World and bought a good-sized farm in New York in 1859. He was naturalized as a member of that colony and married an American woman. He prospered and took up writing about American life; his writing, *Letters from an American Farmer*, was well received. In the late 1790s, Crèvecoeur returned to France and died there. Were it not for the truth in it, his writing might be dismissed as incurably fulsome. And too, it was not altogether complimentary. When his travels took him to Charleston, South Carolina, he noted a bad mentality. Of an upper-class in

---

19. The comments and documents cited in connection with the inception of democratic government at Jamestown are for the most part found in Warren Billings, ed., *The Old Dominion in the Seventeenth Century: A Documentary History of Virginia, 1606–1689* (1975). Other sources are John Smith, *Advertisements for the Inexperienced Planters of New England, or Anywhere or the Pathway to Experience to Erect a Plantation*, Chapter I (1631) and Ralph Hamor, *A True Discourse of the Present Estate of Virginia, and the Successes of the Affaires There till the 18 of Iune. 1614*, available at http://memory.loc.gov

that city, he noted "Their ears by habit are become deaf, their hearts are hardened; they neither see, hear, nor feel for the woes of their poor slaves, from whose painful labours all their wealth proceeds."

Otherwise, Crèvecoeur had different perceptions of what he saw as prevailing conditions of equality and wealth in America. Here he is noteworthy if for no other reason than a particular turn of words, as follows:

> *He* is an American, who, leaving behind him all his ancient prejudices and manners, receives new ones from the new mode of life he has embraced, the new government he obeys, and the new rank he holds. He becomes an American by being received in the broad lap of our great *Alma Mater.* Here individuals of all nations are melted into a new race of men, whose labours and posterity will one day cause great changes in the world.

In fact, the statement "[W]hose labours and posterity will one day cause great changes in the world" is true. But the greatly remembered words out of this passage are that "individuals of all nations are melted into a new race of men."

Out of these words we speak of the melting pot. The action that Crèvecoeur discerned in this vessel was regeneration, saying that "everything has tended to regenerate them . . . new laws, a new mode of living, a new social system." And "here they become men," meaning that with regeneration some better possibilities of human nature were realized. Regeneration of this sort had been spoken of before, as by civic humanists writing of the changed-for-the-better character of persons who amidst feudal Europe had left that society in favor of democratic living in the city states of northern Italy. All of these references are correct, so long as we remember that rejuvenation rather than creation is the action: The spark seen at Athens had always been there; it just needed oxygen as now provided by settlements in North America.

A part of that spark that Crèvecoeur especially discerned was a particular trait, self-interest, and of that trait he saw the good side. He saw the energy and leveling force imparted as self-interest was freed. At Jamestown and Plymouth, free markets had supplanted the initially communistic arrangements in those places and when Crèvecoeur wrote they were entrenched. About the American he wrote, "his labour is founded on the basis of nature, *self-interest;* can it want a stronger allurement?" We had become a people "animated," Crèvecoeur said, by a "spirit of industry, which is unfettered and unrestrained because each person works for himself." In America, individuals owned the produce of their work, "without any part being claimed, either by a despotic prince, a rich abbot, or a mighty lord." Inasmuch as "the rewards of his industry follow with equal steps the progress of his labour," we had left behind much of the "idleness, servile dependence, penury, and useless labour," characteristic of the subjects of old world monarchies. Crèvecoeur knew about old world class systems. And he knew that in America and under its new force of economic freedom, identified as self-interest, the class separations of those old systems had been diminished, his observation being that the "rich and the poor are not so removed from each other as they are in Europe." For the intellectual history of the citizen, Crèvecoeur thus added points, about the energy and leveling force of self-interest, not so much made by Aristotle or civic humanists.

Not much about human capacities is simple, though, so that while self-interest has good points, it may also be destructive, as in service of their own interest imperfect people do cheat or become free riders and such. Accordingly, to self-interest a qualifier was soon added, now by Tocqueville, the other French commentator on America. That qualifier was "rightfully understood." Today, this qualifier may be restated, and properly so, as enlightened or rational self-interest. For the most part, the idea of enlightened self-interest is obvious and simple: As in: people distinguish between honest and cheating companies, merchants, or workers, and reward or rebuke them accordingly, rebuke in the least by refusing to deal with them. Enlightened self-interest takes this into account and nudges all away from purely selfish and dishonest action and all toward trust and beneficial interaction. (As stated by David Hume, "Hence I learn to do a service to another, without bearing him any real kindness; because I foresee, that he will return my service, in expectation of another of the same kind, and in order to maintain the same correspondence of good offices with me and with others.") But then this too is too simple. People cannot always know enough to act that rationally. They cannot know enough to play out how seemingly selfless action is in the end particularly beneficial to them.

Moreover and as we know, people at times do sacrifice themselves for others, do aid others even when they know there is no personal gain. As said by Tocqueville, "It would be very insufficient," he said, "if the principle of self-interest rightly understood had nothing but the present world in view." "Nothing but the present world in view" contrasts material with moral rewards and requires that actions be taken because they are felt as right and not out of sometimes impossible calculations of personal benefit. This reification of self-interest comes back to the quality of citizens stated by Aristotle, of them living well by living virtuously. To this quality and the natural basis of it, we read in Chapter 7 regarding the civic minimum.

In the meantime, though, let me add a note about free market (rather than state-ordered) relations as had begun in America and about "chasing rabbits" as mentioned at the start of this chapter. As had been said by

Rousseau, "If it was a matter of hunting deer everyone well realized that he must remain faithfully at his post; but if a hare happened to pass within reach of one of them, we cannot doubt that he would have gone off in pursuit of it." That thought has become a centerpiece of modern inquiry, under the heading of the stag hunt, on how to maintain beneficial relations in modern societies, the *Stag Hunt and the Evolution of Social Structure* by Brian Skyrms being an instance of this work. A point of Skyrms' work is that the viability of a civic order turns on an evolved trust.

Whether the hunter stays at his post is not wholly a factor of selfishness versus commitment to the common good; life is more complicated than that. If the hunter cannot trust his comrades, that commitment is fruitless and will not be forthcoming, no matter how selfless the hunter may be. Assign rabbits a value of 2 and assume that any hunter can capture one should it happen by. Assign a share of a stag the greater value of 3. However, to gain that greater value each hunter must stay at his post, drawing a circle tight about the prey. Within that circle, if a rabbit happens by, a hunter must choose whether to take that gain or stay at his post on the chance of the greater gain, individually and mutually, of the stag. The choice to the hunter, then, is between the rabbit that may surely be taken and the stag of greater value but subject to the risk of other hunters leaving their post, chasing their own rabbits, and spoiling the hunt. Out of elaborate modeling through game theory and as presented by Skyrms, the outcome is disappointing in that hunters tend to take the rabbit. They tend not to stay together or cooperate. They instead become rabbit hunters and settle for lesser returns, for themselves and their community. (In the terminology of Athens, they were *idiotes*.) Skymrs refers to this outcome as the state of nature. The different state, more adventurous and where people work together for greater returns, he posits as the social contract. As said by Skymrs, "the problem of instituting . . . the social contract can be thought of as the problem of moving from the riskless hunt hare equilibrium to the risky but rewarding stag hunt equilibrium." As conceived, the issue is moving from a state of nature to one of social contract, for us it is that of a citizenry.

Essential to this movement is trust; you must trust others to stay at their posts. Exactly how trust is infused in the first place, though, seems not precisely determinable. An interesting finding, though, is that it can turn on chance. One chance reported was the initial character of the community, as in "sometimes the group converges to all stag hunting and sometimes to all hare hunting, depending on the composition of the group." Our good fortune, the social contract achieved, may be owed to the disposition of those women and men at Plymouth and Jamestown. For us, another favorable condition may have been "the seasoning," exceptionally hard times in the New World, for example, to generate thoughtfully collective action. Also, the "far distance of the place" sheltered the civic order that arose on this side of the Atlantic from interference from the other side.

Getting back around to free markets, as they were established here they may well have been initial conditions that helped generate trust. Greed has its play, human beings are not perfect, but on the whole capitalism turns on trust generated by fair dealing. Scholarly work from Adam Smith also emphasizes this point. But the rudiments are obvious anyway. People do not deal with, work for, or invest in people and firms they do not trust, not if they can help it. Consequently, free markets tend to infuse trust. And in this way are complimentary to a citizenry and vice versa. Or as stated by Francis Fukuyama in his well-received book *Trust* (1995), "The greater economic efficiency was not necessarily achieved by rational self-interested individuals but rather by groups of individuals who, because of a preexisting moral community, are able to work together effectively."

# Chapter Three

# Terms of the Debate

The previous chapter presented the classic idea of the citizen and then not an idea but a fact of the citizen as that person emerged in the colonies. The topic now is on a fuller identification of the citizen, as that person is now conceived by us and the world at large.

Today, part of the identification are two different theories of citizenship — *jus soli* and *jus sanguines*. *Jus soli* citizenship is determined territorially, by and only by the national borders within which a person is born. *Jus sanguines* is not about territory but about relation, in particular the affiliation of parents with a nation. By that affiliation citizenship is gained, as Plato said, by "descent from citizen parents." In the world at large, *jus sanguines* is the usual form of citizenship, and today, given modern movements of people, increasingly so. For the United States today, neither theory, *jus soli* or *jus sanguines*, fully describes or prescribes citizenship as set by the Fourteenth Amendment. But yet components of both, territory and affiliation, are part enough of the Amendment to warrant their consideration.

## *Jus Sanguines*

As between *jus soli* and *jus sanguines*, the better provenance goes to *jus sanguines*. (Or as is sometimes and more descriptively said, by "filiation.") At Athens, citizenship was determined by descent from citizen parents, for reasons that seem grounded in the debt a polity owes its citizens and the idea that life within a citizen family inculcates appropriate civic character. Apart from historical practice, *jus sanguines* has a scholarly grounding, in public law as it emerged in the Renaissance, as its scholars then examined the internal structure of sovereignty from a particular standpoint on natural law. This standpoint was that of a rational makeup of nations, which included relations within as well as among nations. As explained by Emir de Vattel in *The Law of Nations*, the body of this law included "the obligations of a people as well towards themselves as towards other nations." The obligations Vattel spoke of were discerned not from supernatural sources but by reference to nature, to human nature as he saw it.[20]

The scholars who produced the body of law — public law — included Jean-Jacques Burlamaqui (1694–1748), who taught and wrote at the University of Geneva; Baron Samuel von Puffendorf (1632–1694), a German jurist and political philosopher; and Vattel (1714–1767), the Swiss diplomat, scholar, and political philosopher whose principal work was *The Law of Nations*. Vattel, in particular, was read in America. On receiving a copy of *The Law of Nations*, Benjamin Franklin thanked Charles William Frederic Dumas for the gift, saying:

> I am much obliged by the kind present you have made us of your edition of Vattel. It came to us in good season, when the circumstances of a rising state make it necessary frequently to consult the law of nations. Accordingly that copy ... has been continually in the hands of the members of our Congress.

The work thus placed in the hands of the Continental Congress and read in the colonies endorsed *jus sanguines*, saying that "As the society cannot exist and perpetuate itself otherwise than by the children of the citizens, those children naturally follow the condition of their fathers, and succeed to all their rights." And further that "The society is supposed to desire this, in consequence of what it owes to its own preservation; and it is presumed, as matter of course, that each citizen, on entering into society, reserves to his children the right of becoming members of it."

---

20. An instance, from Vattel's *The Law of Nations*, of this natural reasoning is: Man is so formed by nature, that he cannot supply all his own wants, but necessarily stands in need of the intercourse and assistance of his fellow-creatures, whether for his immediate preservation, or for the sake of perfecting his nature, and enjoying such a life as is suitable to a rational being. ... Speech enables them to communicate with each other, to give each other mutual assistance, to perfect their reason and knowledge; and having thus become intelligent, they find a thousand methods of preserving themselves, and supplying their wants. Each individual, moreover, is intimately conscious that he can neither live happily nor improve his nature without the intercourse and assistance of others. Since, therefore, nature has thus formed mankind, it is a convincing proof of her intention that they should communicate with, and mutually aid and assist each other.

Vattel viewed citizenship as determined by descent from citizens in terms of fairness and fitness. In terms of fairness, he saw birthright citizenship as just a return for value received: the value being the citizen parents' day-in-day-out contribution to the body politic, the return being the citizenship for their children. In terms of fitness, the relation of parent to child stood to provide tutelage to the child in the ways of citizenship. As Vattel endorsed *jus sanguines* as the basis of birthright citizenship, he excluded *jus soli*. In his words, "to be of the country, it is necessary that a person be born of a father who is a citizen; for, if he is born there of a foreigner, it will be only the place of this birth, and not his country."[21] Accordingly, after France by its revolution rejected its monarchy and (eventually) assumed a republican identity, it rejected *jus soli* as well. In the words of its Tribunat, "It is too unjust and too much an affront to national dignity that the child of a foreigner, born to him while passing through France . . . who has neither resided in or manifested his desire to remain in France, enjoy all the benefits of the civil law."[22]

---

21. *The Law of Nations*, Ch. 2, Prelim. 20 (1758). On *jus sanguines*, Vattel is worth quoting at length, as follows:

The citizens are the members of the civil society; bound to this society by certain duties, and subject to its authority, they equally participate in its advantages. The natives, or natural-born citizens, are those born in the country, of parents who are citizens. As the society cannot exist and perpetuate itself otherwise than by the children of the citizens, those children naturally follow the condition of their fathers, and succeed to all their rights. The society is supposed to desire this, in consequence of what it owes to its own preservation; and it is presumed, as matter of course, that each citizen, on entering into society, reserves to his children the right of becoming members of it. The country of the fathers is therefore that of the children; and these become true citizens merely by their tacit consent. We shall soon see whether, on their coming to the years of discretion, they may renounce their right, and what they owe to the society in which they were born. I say, that, in order to be of the country, it is necessary that a person be born of a father who is a citizen; for, if he is born there of a foreigner, it will be only the place of his birth, and not his country.

22. Burlamaqui was of a similar opinion. In *The Principles of Natural and Politic Law*, he wrote that "the first founders of states, and all those, who afterwards became members thereof, are supposed to have stipulated, that their children and descendants should, at their coming into the world, have the right of enjoying those advantages, which are common to all the members of the state." J. J. Burlamaqui, The Principles of Natural and Politic Law 213–14 (4th ed., 1792). *See* S. Puffendorf, *De Jure Naturae et Gentium*, Book I, Ch. 2, Prelim. 20 (1672). As did the publicists, Justice Story's associated "national character" with birthright citizenship on more than one occasion, as in Shanks v. Dupont, 28 U.S. 242, 245 (1830), or as in Inglis v. Trustees of Sailor's Snug Harbor, 28 U.S. 99, 169 (1930), where he said "Vattel considers the general doctrine to be, that children generally acquire the national character of their parents."

# *Jus Soli*

The provenance of *jus soli* is different. Its remote origin was in feudalism, the *jus feudal,* where *jus soli* described the entitlement of the holder of an estate, the liege lord, to the life-long service of all persons (fiefs) born within it. In a single court case in England, in 1608, whose long title is *The Union of the Realm of Scotland* and the short and usual title is *Calvin's Case,* this part of feudalism was adopted in service of the English monarchy.[23] The rule of *Calvin's Case* is that anyone born within the king's realm is unalterably and for life the king's subject.

To be sure, *Calvin's Case* had some coverage in the introduction, but the case had several parts. As said by Lord Coke in *Calvin's Case,* the decision was "the longest and weightiest that ever was argued in any Court, the longest in substance . . . the weightiest for the consequent, both for the present, and for all posterity." And here are the parts.

When Queen Elizabeth died without an immediate heir, perhaps leaving the throne vacant, James VI, her distant cousin and king of Scotland, was asked to succeed her, and he did under the new title of James I. This hereditary succession and unification of the two nations by means of the "Union of Crowns" had little support in either populace and a better legitimatization was sought. Given that the Union was not favored by Parliament approbation was not forthcoming from it. Consequently, proponents of the Union of Crowns went over the heads of Parliament, to the courts where they laid claim to a law said to be of divine origin and that as such superseded whatever Parliament and people might otherwise wish or do.

The courts were engaged by means of a child, one Calvin, who claimed title to land located in England and title to that which could be claimed only by an English subject. Calvin had born in Scotland and had spent the first years of his life there. For this reason, he was said to a subject of that nation rather than of England. On the part of the real party in interest, the Crown, this argument was countered as it was said to involve a fundamental error. The error was supposing that a person was born subject to a nation rather than a king.

In Scotland, Calvin had been born under the rule of James during his reign in that nation. The argument presented in *Calvin's Case* was that as prescribed by heaven — one was born subject to the person of a king (James) and not to a (lesser) entity such as a nation. Calvin was born as a subject of James, and not of Scotland or England as either might be represented by a parliament. James had, in his own work *The Trew Law,* posited

---

23. Calvin v. Smith, 77 Eng. Rep. 377 (K.B. 1608).

that a king owns his realm and those in it, the same as a feudal lord owns his fief. In his words, this arrangement arose "before any estates or ranks of men, before any parliaments were holden, or laws made. . . . And so it follows of necessity that kings were the authors and makers of the laws, and not the laws of the kings." (James was an educated man and a writer; *The Trew Law* was one of his several works. Still, about him the slight that stuck was "the wisest fool in Christendom.")

James spoke of kings as "the breathing images of God on earth." Lord Coke's opinion in *Calvin's Case* adhered to that image. In the words of Coke, the heavens infused into all persons born in the king's realm a "ligeance, faith, and obedience to the creation of the Almighty God," whose creation was the king himself. These propositions made the case that at and by birth a person was consigned to subjectship, a servitude to the king within whose realm the person was born. As pronounced by Coke, ligeance and obedience was "an incident inseparable to every subject, for as soon as he is born he oweth by birth-right ligeance and obedience." As Calvin was born in James' realm (then Scotland), he was born James' subject, which subjectship continued wherever the king's territory might spread. As James extended his realm to England, Calvin remained a subject of James, and as a subject he could hold title to land in England inasmuch as it now belonged to James. As did Calvin: The subjectship ascribed to Calvin himself was permanent, it was imposed unalterably and for life. As pronounced by Lord Coke, the "natural ligeance and obedience of the subject cannot be altered."[24]

As it turned on "ligeance and obedience," *Calvin's Case* was of a cloth cut from a feudalist society. As explained by no less than a jurist and historian William Blackstone, the rule of that case had been "derived to us from our Gothic ancestors" and their "feodal system." In time, this cloth became the fabric of the British Empire; as it assured by "dreade," that is by law and superstition, subjection wherever the Empire might spread.[25] James I especially appreciated the psychology; he propounded that "the mysterie of the King's power, is not lawfull to be disputed; for that is to wade into the weaknesse of Princes, and to take away the mysticall reverence." As such and as said in William Holdsworth's *A History of English Law*, *Calvin's Case* "played no small part in consolidating the position of

---

24. Calvin v. Smith, 77 Eng. Rep. at 407. Birthright citizenship by means of *jus soli* is often spoken of a transaction, where the subject's loyalty and service is given in consideration for the protection of the king. But that is not the case. *Jus soli* entails no transactions. The subjects' obedience and the Crown's corollary duty to protect them are externally and divinely imposed and without regard to agreement by anyone.

25. On superstition, *see* Jerome Friedman, *The Battle of the Frogs and Fairford's Flies: Miracles and the Pulp Press During the English Revolution* (1993).

the king as the head and main bond of union between the confederation of independent communities, which now constitute the British Empire."

But as the sun set on the British Empire, it expunged the *Calvin's Case* basis of the realm. In today's United Kingdom, a place more of "citizens" rather than subjects and of modern travel and movements of people, *Calvin's Case* is an anachronism. In 1981, and by means of the British Nationality Act, the United Kingdom supplanted the *Calvin's Case*/territorial measure of citizenship with a portion of *jus sanguines,* of descent from citizen parents, the portion being added better to assure a genuine connection with the Kingdom. Accordingly, the Act provided that birthright citizenship was available only to children born to "British citizens" or to persons "settled in the United Kingdom." At the same time, persons transiently present or present in violation of immigration law were excluded from such citizenship. Most recently, in 2004, *jus soli* was similarly abandoned in Ireland, formerly a part of the Empire, by a national referendum in which 79% of the voters favored the requirement that for birthright citizenship the parent must be an Irish citizen or a legal resident. In other parts of the old empire — Australia, India, and New Zealand — *jus soli* has also been supplanted.[26]

## Consent, Tacit Consent, and Fairness

In their considerable book, *Citizenship Without Consent,* Peter Schuck and Rogers Smith wrote against the rule of *Calvin's Case* and did so from the standpoint of consent, the liberal idea of government by consent. In terms of philosophical provenance, this standard of consent is attributed to John Locke, who famously stated that "a person being born naturally free and equal" does not put himself under the "dominion" of another except "by his own consent." Consent as thus conceived must be mutual, entailing agreement between the person who would be a citizen and the citizenry as a whole.[27] A person must want to be a citizen and the citizenry must accept

---

26. For the United Kingdom, the British Nationality Act of 1981, c. 61, Sec. 1; for Australia, the Australian Citizenship Amendment Act, 1986, Ch. 70, Sec. 7; for India, *The Citizenship Act 1986 amending the Citizenship Act 1955*; for Ireland, the Irish Nationality and Citizenship Act, 2004 (Act No. 38, 2004); and for New Zealand, the Citizenship Amendment Act, 2005 S.N.Z No. 43.

27. In relation to dominion, that of one person over another, the fact that consent to citizenship need be mutual may not be wholly obvious. In the case of a person joined to a nation, consent by that person is patently essential in that he cannot fairly be put under the laws and duties of that nation, under that sort of dominion, except by

her as such. Thus presented, consent usefully identifies the volitional quality of citizenship, which directly contradicts the subjectship coercively imposed by *jus soli* under *Calvin's Case*. *Citizenship Without Consent* makes the case that imposed membership in a nation is inconsistent with democratic citizenship and thus it could not be, as by *Calvin's Case*, a basis of citizenship in a democracy. That being the case, the Fourteenth Amendment could not and did not adopt *jus soli* as the measure of birthright citizenship. But while the principle of consent eliminates *Calvin's Case* as a basis for birthright citizenship in the United States, which is a significant scholarly accomplishment, the principle does not further and fully explain exactly how that citizenship is instead acquired. The question remains of exactly what are the terms of consent set by the Fourteenth Amendment.

A pointer toward the answer, I think, is provided by a somewhat contrived, as by Locke himself, notion of consent, known as "tacit consent." Tacit consent shows up in answer to some ordinary questions about nations, such as the following: May a nation rightfully refuse — on grounds it has not consented — to extend the protection of its law to its visitors? Or, can a person come into a nation and presume not to be bound by its laws because he has not consented? For both questions, the answer is no. For moral and commercial reasons (tourism and business and such), a nation is obliged to protect any person who comes within it. In return, that person is obliged to abide by that nation's law while within it. That is the substantial answer; the short answer is "tacit consent," as follows: by entering a nation, a person tacitly consents to its law. (Locke thus used tacit consent to explain a visitor's obligation to obey the laws of a host nation.[28])

---

his consent. But how is that in terms of dominion a citizenry need consent to the admission of that person? Because a citizenry is an order of power that is shared by its members, a new citizen gains a quantum of power over the other citizens. Within a citizenry, a person is at once under and over fellow citizens. Of course, with one new citizen the power thus gained is infinitesimal. But as the number of new citizens is aggregated over time or increased by an en masse admission of new citizens, the power gained can be considerable. Accordingly and in terms of dominion, a citizenry need consent to the admission of new members.

28. As said by Locke, "The difficulty is, what ought to looked upon as tacit consent, and how far it binds. . . . [E]very man that has any possession or enjoyment of any part of the dominions of any government does thereby give his tacit consent and is as far forth obliged to obedience to the laws of that government during such enjoyment, as anyone under it. . . ." John Locke, *The Second Treatise of Government* (1689), Ch. VII, para. 119. In the United States, John Marshall in Schooner Exchange v. McFaddon, 11 U.S. 116, 144 (1812) explained, not in terms of consent but in terms of reciprocal moral and economic relations, that a nation is obliged to protect any person that comes

Tacit consent, however, is not consent. It is something of a homonym, perhaps, but it is not consent. Properly speaking, consent is subjective; it is an internal, within the mind, state of agreement. "Tacit consent" is not that; rather, it is an outcome objectively determined by reference to an exogenous set of facts. For instance, in 1648 the Laws and Liberties of Massachusetts provided that "in putting your persons and estates into the protection . . . held forth and exercised within this jurisdiction, you doe tacitly consent to this government and to all the wholesome lawes thereof." Here, tacit consent does not depict subjective agreement but rather a condition of fairness objectively determined. The condition being that one could not fairly accept the benefits of law as provided by Massachusetts without at the same time abiding by that law. On the point of birthright citizenship, Vattel observed that the children of citizens "become true citizens merely by their tacit consent," which is not consent but instead a statement of the fairness in passing the parents' citizenship on to their children.

In the way that fairness is central to tacit consent, fairness is central to birthright citizenship in the United States. Consider again the circumstances of the *Wong Kim Ark* case (United States v. Wong Kim Ark, 169 U.S. 649 (1898)): Could the people of the United States invite Chinese immigrants to this country to work and live out their lives here, as we had by the Burlingame Treaty and then fairly refuse — as that treaty did — to provide citizenship to their children born here? We could not and thus fairness — fairness as reciprocity — was at work in that case. Although actual consent may not readily explain birthright citizenship under *Wong Kim Ark* case, tacit consent in the form of fairness does do so.

---

within it and that it return by that nations law. This matter of reciprocal obligations that is the substance of tacit was visited in debate in Congress on birthright citizenship under the Fourteenth Amendment. See Chapter 5 on the subject.

# Chapter Four

# The Citizen in the Original Constitution

In 1776 and on the eve of the Revolutionary War, we knew we were not subjects. But if not that who were we? If not bound to the English Crown, we were bound to the King's language and in that language there was no word for us. Consequently, at the start of 1776 the Continental Congress simply referred to us as "inhabitants," as in the "Inhabitants of the Colonies."

However, in England there had been a small and limited and idiomatic use of a certain word, to not to refer to the people of a nation but instead to the residents of a city, and just and only to them. The word of that small usage was "citizen." The word "citi" meant a city or village and "zen" meant a place. Accordingly, a 1776 document referred to one John Wollaston, as a "cittizen & Goldsmith of London." As the Revolution approached, the usage of citizen, as a resident of a city or town, was to the "citizens" of Boston, which was then occupied by the British military. For example, in the summer of 1775 the Continental Congress referred to Boston's "thirty thousand citizens subjected to all the miseries attending so sudden a convulsion in their commercial metropolis."

Although these communiqués were about citizens in the small sense of municipal residents, there was yet in them a rising sense of us as a whole, the colonies collectively as we gathered as a people. In this way, the linguistic arc of the word *citizen* was on the rise, away from municipality and toward a people. In a resolution against British action in Boston, the Continental Congress verbally and spiritually associated "the free citizens of Boston" with the "honour and safety of a free people." With that linkage, the word *citizen* included the 2.5 million people spreading from South Carolina to Massachusetts. In the late spring of 1776, the arc was completed, so that citizen could be referred to and distinguished us as a people. The first public statement of this new sense of citizen may well have been by Thomas Paine, in his sensational publication of *Common Sense* (1776), in which he called on us not dully as inhabitants but more gloriously as citizens.

Shortly thereafter, on July 4, 1776, the word *citizen* made its first appearance in a public document, Declaration of Independence as it spoke to "fellow Citizens." Thereafter, in the Continental Congress its former references to inhabitants were replaced by citizens. On August 1, 1776, Dr. Benjamin Rush, physician, educator, and delegate from Pennsylvania, addressing the Continental Congress in Independence Hall, proclaimed: "I would not have it understood that I am pleading the cause of Pennsylvania; when I entered that door, I considered myself a citizen of America."[29]

In the colonies, then, we conceived of citizen in a new and different way. As the word was now conceived, it was deployed in various places in the 1787 Constitution. For instances, the "Privileges and Immunities of Citizens", Article IV, Section 2, spoke of us as "citizens" in the United States, and by Article I members of the Senate had to be a citizen. But as the word was not used, it was not defined. The 1787 Constitution said we were citizens but provided no conceptual seating for the term. A seating might have been provided, as by the Massachusetts' Constitution of 1780. That state constitution provided that "The body politic is formed by a voluntary association of individuals, it is a social compact, by which the whole people covenants with each citizen, and each citizen with the whole people, that all shall be government by certain laws for the common good."

Although it did not much identify the citizen, the Constitution did have provisions that helped establish the citizens as a sustainer. The First Amendment of 1791 protected freedoms of speech, press, and assembly as are essential to self-government in a republic. That same Amendment precluded the national church that is characteristic of a subjugated society. The main Constitution, as Article I, Section 9, cl. 8 provided that "No Title of Nobility shall be granted by the United States," precluded a hereditary aristocracy. The Second Amendment's "right to bear arms" precluded an instance of aristocracy, that it might bear arms while the peasantry could not. The

---

29. Journals of the Continental Congress, 1774–1789 (July 28, 1775). Shortly after its inaugural appearance in the Declaration of Independence, "citizen" was used in contradistinction to subjects in a draft of a treaty of friendship with France, as that draft referred to "Subjects of the said most Christian King [of France]" and "Citizens of the said United States." As regards the French, "citoyen" was a password in the French Revolution. Ton Van Eyden, *Public Management of Society* (2003) refers to "the invention of the concept of citoyen in 1789." Thurston Greene, *The Language of the Constitution*, 117 (1991), in its entry on "citizen," is a useful reference; the reference to John Wollaston, as a "cittizen & Goldsmith of London," is from it.

most debated, contested, and defined provisions of the Constitution, the federalism that preserved state and local government, provided spaces where citizens might more actively participate in government and better develop civic competency.

But while mindful of the citizen, the 1787 Constitution failed to identify the person. A reason, of course, was "the difficult question of the status of Negro slaves." For African Americans, the status was that they were not nor could be citizens. It took civil war and the Fourteenth Amendment to make them citizens. But until the Fourteenth Amendment, even the full identity of white people had to be worked out.

## Fundamental Law

The fact that the Constitution of 1787 was short on definition of the citizen did not mean that fundamental understandings about the person — in an ongoing republic there had to be — were not in place. Consistent with ordinary expectations and public law, the original body of citizens was the generation — the "We the People" — denoted in the Constitution's first sentence, and that sentence is identified as having "establish[ed]" the Constitution. The Supreme Court has declared as much on various occasions, saying that "The words 'people of the United States' and 'citizens' are synonymous" and "both describe the political body who . . . form the sovereignty, and who hold the power and conduct the government through their representatives."[30]

In the antebellum years, there was little in the way of scholarly comment — at least from American authors — respecting birthright citizenship. Instead, commentary from abroad was mostly read, especially Vattel's *The Law of Nations* (1758) and its idea that the child followed the "national character" of the parents in particular. Commentary from this side of the Atlantic was sketchy, and provided in the work of William Rawle, Joseph Story, and James Kent. Apart from scholarly commentary, Story and Kent had distinguished judicial careers, and for Story the more extensive consideration of birthright citizenship was in his Supreme Court opinions rather than his commentary. Kent, though, also had his moment from the bench, as is shown in *Goodell v. Jackson*.

Rawle produced our first treatise on the Constitution, which work bears very few comments about birthright citizenship. The founding generation, he wrote, comprised the original citizenry and thereafter this citizenry was

---

30. Boyd v. Nebraska, 143 U.S. 135, 159 (1892).

continued by their descendants. This was a natural and reasonable expectation, he said, that we were bound to respect. In his words:

> No one can suppose that the parent intended . . . his children should not partake of the same rights, enjoy the same liberty, and be protected by the same government. Nature itself impresses on the parental mind, a desire to promote the interests of children. . . . The pleasing sensation in the parent, of passing from the condition of an oppressed subject, to that of a citizen of a free republic, would surely be impaired by a consideration that his offspring would acquire no birthright in the community of his choice.[31]

The more influential commentators were Joseph Story and James Kent, both as jurists and scholars. Of the two, Kent in his scholarly hat and by a single sentence in a footnote said, "Citizens, under our Constitution and laws, mean free inhabitants, born within the United States." As a judge, though, Kent was not so rigid. In *Goodell v. Jackson,* he found that a person could be born within the United States and not be a citizen.

In *Goodell v. Jackson,* William Sagoharase was a Native American of the Oneida Tribe, and he claimed to be a citizen. Had birth in the United States been the rule, the case would have been easy; Sagoharase was indeed born in the United States. But as said by Chancellor Kent, "mere territorial jurisdiction" was in this case an insufficient basis of birthright citizenship. In the case at hand for tribal Native Americans, the better question was "whether they have become amalgamated with us, and incorporated into the body politic." As asked by Kent, are Native Americans under tribal government charged with the duties and burdens of citizens? "Do they pay taxes, or serve in the militia, or are they required to take a share in any of the details of our local institutions?"

The question put to the court in *Goodell v. Jackson* had not been "whether [tribal Native American] reside within our territory or jurisdiction; but whether they form a part of the body politic, or people of the state." As the case turned not on territory but on identification with the body politic, it

---

31. William Rawle, *A View of the Constitution of the United States,* 84–101 (2nd ed. 1829). The public law he followed had been succinctly stated by Burlamaqui, in his statement previously noted, that "[T]he first founder of state, and all those who afterwards became members thereof, are supposed to have stipulated, that their children and descendants should, at their coming into the world, have the right of enjoying those advantages which are common to all the members of the state." J. J. Burlamaqui, *The Principles of Natural and Politic Law,* 213–14 (4th ed. 1792).

foreshadowed "subject to the jurisdiction" as that clause became a qualifier of the Fourteenth Amendment.[32]

Story was fairly consistent on citizenship. In his commentary he was discerning about *Calvin's Case* (as summarized in Chapter 1), as it stood for subjectship in Great Britain, but in his work on the Supreme Court he rejected the decision. In his commentary he noted that "persons who are born in a country are generally deemed to be citizens and subjects of that country." But immediately he added a qualifier altogether inconsistent with *Calvin's Case*. As added by Story, "A reasonable qualification of this rule would seem to be that it should not apply to the children of parents who were *in itinere* in the country or who were abiding there for temporary purposes."[33] That was Story in his commentary. On the bench he spoke more extensively. In Supreme Court opinions he posited fitness, the child "doeth partake of the national character" of the parents[34] rather than the territory where the child was born, as determinative of birthright citizenship. To these opinions, we shortly turn.

In contrast to perfunctory withdrawals from the handy language bank of Great Britain, an explanation of substance, or seemingly so, was in antebellum America offered for the *Calvin's Case* basis. The explanation was reciprocity and it worked this way: The sovereign provides the protection of law; in return for that protection the subject gives "ligeance and obedience." There are, however, problems with this notion. When a thug tells a shop owner he will protect the shop's business in return for a weekly payment from the owner, perhaps we might describe that payment, given as it is in return for protection, as "reciprocity." But of course, we do not. We instead refer to those payments as extortion. After our Revolution, the British persisted in forcibly seizing American sailors who had been born in England, on the grounds that by *Calvin's Case* those sailors were born as and remained British subjects. We might have viewed those impressments as reciprocity, but we did not. Instead, we viewed those impressments as coercion, and in the War of 1812 we fought against the practice.

---

32. Goodell v. Jackson, 20 Johns. 693 (N.Y. 1823). Kent's statement favoring *jus soli* is at 2 Kent's Commentaries 27 & note.

33. Joseph Story, *Commentaries on the Conflict of Laws*, Sec. 48, at 28 (1834).

34. That the child "doeth partake of the national character" of parents was then and is now used. But as we now speak of children we know that today, as opposed to the early eighteenth century when Story and others spoke, children gain a public education where civics and politics are taught. In the early eighteenth century, there were no such schools.

Used together, reciprocity and *Calvin's Case* are an unenlightening mismatch of concepts. An insight is provided by Justice Story. "The rule commonly laid down," he wrote, "is that every person who is born within the ligeance of a sovereign is a subject." But that rule, he said, "affords no light to guide us in the inquiry what constitutes allegiance ... or ... what are the facts and circumstances from which the law deduces the conclusion of citizenship." A reason the rule afforded no light was that ligeance was already an anachronism, a deficit in the *Calvin's Case* vocabulary. Although allegiance is an important and helpful word respecting citizenship in a republic, ligeance as in *Calvin's Case* is not. The word *allegiance* may proceed from ligeance, but not as you might think. Allegiance is more of a transliteration (a sound alike) than a synonym. Allegiance refers to loyalty and commitments freely given, and such loyalty and commitments are characteristic of a republic. Ligeance is something else; it comes out of feudalism and is the indelible and unalterable duty of obedience owed by the subject to the Crown. Consequently, allegiance and ligeance are more in the order of antonyms than synonyms; allegiance is volitional and ligeance is imposed. Blurring that distinction — thinking "that every person who is born within the ligeance of a sovereign is a subject" identifies the allegiance for which citizenship is given — is a confusion of terms and concepts.

# An Alleged Common Law

Although the Crown it served had been evicted, *Calvin's Case* somehow stayed on in America, or so it is thought. It is said to have remained as a part of English common law, the law we did indeed find some parts useful and kept. A colleague, Professor Polly Price, has written of *Calvin's Case*. In that writing, though, she makes two suppositions about the case's survival in America. These suppositions are (1) that "*Calvin's Case* was one of the most important English common-law decisions adopted by courts in the early history of the United States" and (2) that "Rules of citizenship derived from *Calvin's Case* became the basis of the American common-law rule of birthright citizenship, a rule that was later embodied in the Fourteenth Amendment of the U.S. Constitution."[35] However, it cannot be supposed that *Calvin's Case* "had been adopted by courts in the early history of the United State" and it is doubly wrong to suppose that that the case was "later embodied in the Fourteenth Amendment of the U.S. Constitution."

---

35. Polly J. Price, Natural Law and Birthright Citizenship in Calvin's Case, 9 *Yale J. L. Human.* 73 (1997).

Suppositions that *Calvin's Case* fills in silences in the Constitution on citizenship are out of harmony with the document. A score of republicanism runs through the Constitution within which *Calvin's Case,* conceived as it was to serve the British Crown, is considerably discordant. Presenting *Calvin's Case* as a part of the common law may seem to tone down the dissonance, but then not really. As we absorbed parts of the common law, we (rightly) did so respecting several matters of state and local law as opposed to matters of national power, which is a reason Justice Brandeis is so famously stated in *Erie v. Tompkins,* "There is no federal general common law." Moreover, the states that absorbed parts of the common law largely did so for private relations, matters of contract, tort, property interests, and the like, and primarily placed control of these relations in private hands.

*Calvin's Case* is not that kind of local and private law; instead, it is a matter of a national power of royal character. If it is part of the common law referred to as *jura coronae,* and that law is identified as not right for the United States. St. George Tucker had a long career as a federal and state court judge and before that as a law professor at William and Mary Law School. He wrote and published *Blackstone's Commentaries* with, as he said in the title, *notes of reference to the constitution and laws of the federal government of the United States.* In that work, and as regards the reception of common law in the United States, Tucker distinguished between the part of that law that applied to private relations and the part, the *jura coronae,* as applied to the English Crown. He described "private relations" as "comprehending the rules, maxims, and usages adopted to ensure the legal and uninterrupted enjoyment of a man's life, his limbs, his body, his health, and his reputation." This part, he wrote, might properly be used by the states, as a matter of common law, as it might fit their conditions, and, of course, was so used in contracts and torts.

The *jura corona* was altogether matter. In "contradistinction" to the ordinary common law the states had received, the *jura corona* "rest[ed] upon immemorial usurpations, exactions, and oppressions, generated by feudal tyranny." And as such was not fit for consumption by a republican government. As said by Tucker, "Neither can we suppose the laws which regarded the king as supreme lord of the soil of his dominions . . . would be applicable to the condition of colonists who held their lands in free and common socage." Which rejection was especially apt so in light of and after the Revolution: As regards the Revolution, Tucker wrote:

> [E]very rule of the common law, and every statute of England, founded on the nature of regal government, in derogation of the natural and unalienable rights of mankind; or, inconsistent with the nature and principles of democratic governments, were absolutely abrogated,

repealed, and annulled. . . . This is a natural and necessary consequence of the revolution, and the correspondent changes in the nature
of the governments, unless we could suppose that the laws of England,
like those of the Almighty Ruler of the universe, carry with them an
intrinsic moral obligation upon all mankind. A supposition too gross
and absurd to require refutation.

The incredulity of supposing that we might resort to the common law to
resolve public law matters, citizenship in particular, was seconded by Justice Story in a case, *Shanks v. Dupont,* about birthright citizenship. In that
case and consequent to a determination of birthright citizenship, Story
rejected, as irrelevant, any consideration of *femmes covert,* the common law
status of married women. That law, he explained, did not reach women's
"political rights, nor prevent their acquiring or losing a national character."
Instead, "those rights stand upon the more general principles of the law of
nations." By the law of nations he meant public law. He meant public law as
opposed to common law.

If the common law horse for *Calvin's Case* needs more flogging, consider
this assertion by the Supreme Court in 1829 in *Van Ness v. Pacard*: "The
common law of England is not to be taken in all respects to be that of America. Our ancestors brought with them its general principles . . . but . . . only
that portion which was applicable to their situation." Or consider the
Rhode Island charter, which became its constitution when it joined the
union, as it declared, "The common law of England is not to be taken in all
respects to be that of America. Our ancestors brought with them its general principles . . . but . . . only that portion which was applicable to their
situation." Moreover, the conceptual nucleus of *Calvin's Case,* the doctrine
of perpetual obedience that Lord Coke declared was an "inseparable" part
of English, was visibly and definitively rejected in antebellum American —
rejected because it was wholly out of "harmony with the genius, spirit, and
object of our institutions." One institution was the United States Attorney
General, in an opinion by Attorney General Cushing.

The opinion started with a question that in republican eyes seems
improbable. A Prussian minister asked the United States whether a citizen
could emigrate from the United States to Prussia. Apparently, the Prussian
minister was unsure whether the United States was yet bound by the *Calvin's Case* rule of perpetual allegiance. Accordingly, the minister asked
whether the émigré could "expatriate himself." Attorney General Cushing
replied that of course he could, because in America we were "citizens" rather
than "subjects." Therefore, "The doctrine of absolute and perpetual allegiance — the root of the denial of any right of emigration — is inadmissible
in the United States."

Instead, the United States had from the beginning allowed our citizens to emigrate. We did so by understanding that emigrants can give up their allegiance to the nation and instead owe allegiance to another country. Most dramatically, Cushing's dismissal of perpetual allegiance on the grounds we are citizens rather than subjects, subjects being the subject of *Calvin's Case,* had earlier been evident in our renewed war, the War of 1812, with England. As previously discussed, owing to *Calvin's Case* England had refused to think that its subjects could emigrate to America and thus discard their duty of perpetual obedience to the English Crown. Accordingly, England persisted in impressing them, boarding our vessels and forcibly taking from them sailors who had been born in England. Which practice Thomas Jefferson described as an "extension of colonial submission" and was a cause for the war.

Cushing's opinion was otherwise grounded in our case law. In *Talbot v. Jansen,* decided shortly after the ratification of the Constitution, the owners of a Dutch ship captured by American privateers had sued them for damages. The privateers claimed they were not liable inasmuch as they were not American citizens and thus not subject to claims in a US court. Although they had once been US citizens, defendants argued that they had given it up by means of expatriation. On the side of expatriation, their counsel strenuously argued that the liberty of a citizen included quitting the country. He did so by contrasting that liberty with the premises of *Calvin's Case,* "which . . . chained men to the soil on which they were born; and converted the bulk of mankind into the villeins, or slaves of a lord, or superior. From the feudal system sprung the law of perpetual allegiance." Counsel continued, saying, "Citizenship is the charter of equality; allegiance is a badge of inferiority. Citizenship is constitutional; allegiance is personal. Citizenship is freedom; allegiance is servitude." Our Supreme Court agreed. As said by Justice Iredell, "a man should not be confined against his will to a particular spot, because he happened to draw his first breath upon it" nor "be compelled to continue in a society to which he is accidentally attached."[36]

---

36. Cushing's opinion is at 8 U.S. Op. Atty. Gen. 139 (1856). Talbot v. Jansen, 3 U.S. 133 (1795). Under *Calvin's Case,* expatriation was a serious crime. As described by Justice Fuller in United States v. Wong Kim Ark, 169 U.S. 649, 712 (1898): "Lord Grenville wrote to our minister, Rufus King: 'No British subject can, by such a form of renunciation as that which is prescribed in the American law of naturalization, devest himself of his allegiance to his sovereign. Such a declaration of renunciation made by any of the king's subjects would, instead of operating as a protection to them, be considered an act highly criminal on their part.' 2 Am. St. Papers, 149."

In time, Congress declared that expatriation and emigration rather than perpetual obedience per *Calvin's Case* prevailed in America. Within two weeks of the ratification of the Fourteenth Amendment, that body passed an act declaring that "expatriation is a natural and inherent right." In the words of that enactment, any doctrine to the contrary was "inconsistent with the fundamental principles of this government." In floor debate, Senator Judd of Illinois quickly ended any thought that the common law as might be attributed to *Calvin's Case* somehow stood in opposition to the enactment. There could be no such opposition, he said, because there was no such common law. Although it was true that the states had absorbed some parts of the common law, they had used, Judd explained, only so much of that as it was compatible "with their situation." A *Calvin's Case* portion of the "English common law", he said, was incompatible, being out of "harmony with the genius, spirit, and object of our institutions."[37]

## Congress and the Act of 1790

The original citizenry consisted of the generation that adopted the Constitution and, then their descendants who gained that citizenship as a matter of course. That citizenry, however, was added to by immigration. As immigrants gained citizenship, they did so by naturalization, by law enacted by Congress. Children born to them *after* their naturalization also received citizenship, by being born to them as a citizen. But then, how did children born to immigrants before they were naturalized gain citizenship?

The answer was quickly and positively provided by Congress as that body in its first session enacted the Immigration and Naturalization Act of 1790. On being naturalized, immigrants became citizens. And so did the children born to them before they were naturalized. The 1790 Act provided that upon naturalization of an immigrant, all children "dwelling within the United States shall also be considered as citizens of the United States." To be noted, these children were not made citizens by reference to *Calvin's Case* and place of birth. It mattered not at all whether these children had

---

37. Cong. Globe, 40th Cong., 1st Sess. 969 (1868). The Act is found at 15 Stat. 223, c. 249. The right of expatriation as declared by the Act stood to be qualified by exigent circumstances. No sane nation allows expatriation to be used to avoid just obligations. One should not expatriate so as to run out on a money debt or public duties such as wartime service. Understanding that in Talbot v. Jansen, 3 U.S. at 133, 153–54, Justice Patterson hoped that Congress would enact a statute delineating the right and in time it did.

been born in the United States or abroad. Rather, citizenship turned on the affiliation of their parents' new affiliation with us, on the parents having been naturalized.

That Congress linked citizenship to citizen parents was suggested to be the case by the United States Supreme Court and was held to be the case by New York's highest court. The 1790 Act included the qualification that "the right of citizenship shall not descend to persons whose fathers have never been resident in the United States."[38] In light of this qualification, it appeared to the US Supreme Court, in *Weedin v. Chin Bow*, that the children-born-abroad part of the 1790 Act was not so much meant to establish birthright citizenship for children born abroad as to condition it, by requiring that the parents stay connected with the United States. On this account, the Court quoted Secretary of State Hamilton Fish as he had referred to the "heritable blood of citizenship" and explained that by the 1790 Act that blood was "associated unmistakably with residence within the country." Without a requirement of US residency, the Court noted that generations of citizens might be born and live abroad, in "a family without any relation to the United States" and would have "evaded the duties and responsibilities of American citizenship." (The modern Supreme Court has a similar view of the 1790 Act, as it has explained that the Act's modern version has the "legitimate" purpose of assuring that parents have maintained a meaningful connection with the United States so that the fruits (civic character) of that connection is passed on to their child. As said by the Court and as earlier noted, that connection consists of "the real, everyday ties that provide a connection between child and citizen parent and, in turn, the United States."[39])

The holding in New York, of an overruling standard of descent from citizen parents, was in *Ludlam v. Ludlam*, the facts of which are a bit complicated. In 1802, Congress reenacted the 1790 Act and its provision respecting children born abroad. Inadvertently it seems, as reenacted the statue precluded citizenship to children born abroad to parents who had become citizens after 1802. In time, this error was cured, but in a meantime of

---

38. In its entirety, the 1790 Act, as it pertained to children born abroad, provided: "And the children of citizens of the United States, that may be born beyond sea, or out of the limits of the United States, shall be considered as natural-born citizens: Provided, that the right of citizenship shall not descend to persons whose fathers have never been resident in the United States." 1 Stat. 103 (1790).

39. Weedin v. Chin Bow, 274 U.S. 657, 666–67 (1927). The modern Supreme Court statement about connecting the parents and through them the child to United States is at Tuan Anh Nguyen v. Immigration & Naturalization Service, 533 U.S 53, 65 (2001).

about fifty years children born abroad to persons who had become citizens after 1802 could not, at least under the Act, gain birthright citizenship. Did this mean that these children were not born as citizens?

This question was heard by the New York Court of Appeal in the *Ludlam v. Ludlam* case and the answer of the court was that these children were indeed born as citizens, not by means of the 1790 Act but instead by operation of fundamental law. As found by the court, they were born as citizens because descent from citizen parents, as opposed to the geographic fact of birth on US soil, was the underlying rule. In the words of the court, birthright citizenship "does not depend upon the boundaries of the place, as *Calvin's Case* asserts." Instead, birthright citizenship was determined by descent from citizen parents. As said by the court, citizenship "must be . . . transmitted from parents to the child or it could not exist."[40] This holding, obviously, is altogether contrary to the assumption that *Calvin's Case* and birthright citizenship as determined by location of birth prevailed in America.

# Antebellum Case Law

Where birthright citizenship did not work well or at all in antebellum America was for African Americans. They were denied citizenship by any means, by birthright or by naturalization, and that denial led to war and the reconstitution of our citizenship by the Fourteenth Amendment. Apart from the egregious exclusion of African Americans, though, the antebellum system of citizenship seems to have been capacious enough to include most if not all of those of a good connection to the nation.

By that system, the status of citizen passed to descendants of citizens, whether the descendant was born here or abroad, or by the Immigration and Naturalization Act of 1790 to children of immigrants. But neither category, descendent from a citizen or as the child of a naturalized citizen, provided little of a stress line along which a line of cases respecting birthright citizenship might develop. Although there was not much of a stress line, there were a few points of pressure.

One point of pressure was time limited, involving circumstances of the Revolutionary War. A second point was the infrequent matter of birth on US soil to persons from abroad who did not become naturalized citizens. A third point involved the time warp, the fifty-year gap in the coverage of the 1790 Act for children born abroad to US citizens. (A fourth point, as to

---

40. Ludlam v. Ludlam, 26 N.Y. 356, 364 (1863).

which I defer discussion until the chapter on the Fourteenth Amendment, pertained to Native Americans and for whom the law inasmuch as it had then crystallized was that those who lived under tribal government were not entitled to birthright citizenship, where those who left that government and lived among us and in the manner of citizens gained it, as indicated in the Chancellor Kent opinion in *Goodell v. Jackson.*)

The stress points produced a half of a dozen decisions. Scoring the cases strictly by a convention of *Calvin's Case* versus the public law (relation of parents to the child) favors public law. On the whole, though, these decisions are better viewed as being pragmatic rather than doctrinal. By pragmatic I mean in particular that the courts considered how "national character" might be best inculcated through birthright citizenship and otherwise looked to various matters of national policy such as treaty obligations.

In a pair of cases decided in 1830, *Shanks v. Dupont* and *Inglis v. Trustees of Sailor's Snug Harbour,* the Supreme Court considered the complicated circumstances of the citizenship of children born at the time of the Revolution. Had *Calvin's Case* been faithfully applied, both cases would have been easy. As the persons in question were born within the reign of King George, then by *Calvin's Case* they were born as British subjects and remained so for life. But our Revolution upset the order of *Calvin's Case.* A new order was established by the Declaration of Independence as it asserted that that "these united colonies are, and of right ought to be, free and independent states; that they are absolved from all allegiance to the British crown." With that assertion, the ligeance owed the Crown by those loyal to the American cause was dissolved. In the place of that "ligeance," they instead became citizens of our newly formed nation. In terms of birthright citizenship, the rule laid down was that children born before July 4, 1776 were born as British subjects. But while persons born before July 4, 1776 were born as British subjects, their subjectship changed over to our citizenship after July 4 if they elected to adhere to the American cause, and election was presumed as they lived here as citizens. Stated differently, those born in the colonies as British subjects became our citizens after July 4, 1776 unless they visibly opted out.[41]

This context framed the disputes about citizenship in *Shanks v. Dupont* and *Inglis v. Trustees of Sailor's Snug Harbor.* Both cases involved ownership

---

41. An exegesis of this development, from "[b]efore the revolution" when "all the colonies constituted a part of the dominions of the king of Great Britain, and all the colonists were natural born subjects" to a conversion to American citizenship by means of the Revolution, is provided by Justice Story's opinion in Inglis v. Trustees of Sailor's Snug Harbor, 28 U.S. 99,157ff (1830).

of real property. In *Shanks v. Dupont*, the majority opinion was by Justice Story, who paid attention to national character as determined by parentage.[42] One justice dissented on *Calvin's Case* grounds of perpetual allegiance, but that was a dissent not the opinion of the Court. The property in *Shanks v. Dupont* (an inheritance of land in South Carolina) was subject to the Treaty of 1794 (the "Jay Treaty") between England and the United States as it protected the interests of British subjects in property they might own in the United States. Consequently, were Ms. Shanks a British subject at the time she made the will in question her property in South Carolina was protected by the treaty and properly conveyed by her will.

Ms. Shanks had been born in Charleston at some indeterminate time before July 4, 1776 to parents who were "confirmed American loyalists." In 1782, she married an English officer during the British occupation of Charleston and went with him to England when that occupation ended. Thereafter, in England she made the will that conveyed the property in South Carolina. Under the Jay Treaty, this conveyance was valid, if she were a British subject when she made the will.

When Ms. Shank was born, South Carolina had been a British colony, and thus by *Calvin's Case* faithfully applied, she was born as and forever was a British subject. But that case, overturned as it was by the American Revolution, was not so applied. Consequently, even though she was born a British subject, that status changed to US citizenship — if she had so elected by means of her allegiance to the American cause at the time of the Revolution. Her age at the time of the Revolution, though, was unknown, so a question of fact, perhaps, was whether she was sufficiently mature to make the election. As explained by Justice Story, if she were "of age" then "her birth and residence might be deemed to make her, by means of her election, a United States citizen." Be that as it may, if she were not of age she was still a US citizen; under public law (not common law per *Calvin's Case* but public law) as a child, she did "partake of the national character" of her parents. Her father the confirmed loyalist was unquestionably a US citizen. Accordingly and per Justice Story, "If she was not of age, then she might well be deemed ... to hold the citizenship of her father; for children ... partake of his national character, as a citizen of that country."

However sliced, either by her election if she were of age or by her absorbing the national character of her parents, Ms. Shanks was a US citizen. (All of which denied *Calvin's Case*.) But in the end, she was found not to have been a citizen at the time that counted most, which was when she wrote

---

42. Shanks v. Dupont, 28 U.S. 242 (1830).

the will that conveyed the property in question. She had written it in England, well after she departed Charleston with her English husband to thereafter live in England. For Justice Story, this move to England with her English husband was taken to be another election, this time to be an English subject. By that election, Ms. Shanks had changed her US citizenship to English subjectship, and under the Jay Treaty her children got the property.

Everything considered, the Court's reasoning in the case, if consistent with a particular typology, was consistent with public law. Her American parents counted in establishing her "character" as an American citizen. Thereafter and in accordance with our notions of volitional citizenship as opposed to the perpetual ligeance of *Calvin's Case*, her choice to take up a new life in England counted. The fact *Calvin's Case* had been no part of the decision was emphasized by the dissent. In dissent, Justice Johnson denied the volitional nature of citizenship. He said that "Mrs. Shanks continued, as she was", a US citizen, because citizenship was "unalienable." (Justice Johnson was consistent in his adherence to *Calvin's Case* and hence consistently in the minority, as in the *Inglis v. Trustees of Sailor's Snug Harbor* case.) Otherwise, pragmatism rather than doctrinal purity was at work in the majority opinion in *Shanks v. Dupont*. Justice Story looked to sources as were applicable or useful; he carefully took into account the "spirit and intent" of the Jay Treaty and, as he said, of "public law."[43]

The second case, *Inglis v. Trustees of Sailor's Snug Harbor*, is lengthy, variously reasoned, productive of conflicting quotes, and resistant of concise description.[44] John Inglis had been born in the city of New York and was no more than one year of age when British troops entered and occupied the city in 1776. When the British left the city in 1783, his father left with them and took John to England. John Inglis then remained abroad for the rest of his life. In the case before the Court, he claimed a right to inherent certain property (the Snug Harbour home for sailors) in New York. As in the *Shanks v. Dupont* case, his inheritance turned on whether he was a US citizen or a British subject. Under New York law, Inglis need be a US citizen as opposed to a British subject in order to inherent. The lead opinion in the case, by Justice Thompson, was that Inglis was not a US citizen. Because he had

---

43. Otherwise, and as earlier noted, Story found that the common law as it might be used to determine Ms Shanks citizenship according to her marital status had no application, saying that that law did not "reach" her "political rights" nor "prevent [her] acquiring or losing a national character."

44. Inglis v. Trustees of Sailor's Snug Harbor, 28 U.S. at 99.

been born to British subjects, he was himself born a British subject and remained so inasmuch as he had left the United States to live in England. In this respect, Justice Thompson summarized his reasoning as follows:

> The facts disclosed in this case, then, lead irresistibly to the conclusion that it was the fixed determination of Charles Inglis the father, at the declaration of independence, to adhere to his native [British] allegiance. And John Inglis the son must be deemed to have followed the condition of his father, and the character of a British subject attached to and fastened on him also.

Within the case, how the "character of a British subject" attached to John was more fully shown by a matrix complicated by circumstances of the Revolution.[45] But as complicated as that matrix is, the salient point is that by it birthright citizenship was rather more determined by John Inglis having "followed the condition of his father" as opposed to it being "deemed" by place of birth. This public law principle was affirmed by the dissent, by Justice Johnson who again objected on *Calvin's Case* grounds. By Johnson's reasoning, place of birth alone determined citizenship. And that status once acquired could not, under the doctrine of perpetual allegiance, be changed by the individual's election or otherwise. As said by Johnson, "the

---

45. Inglis had been born in New York around the start of the Revolutionary War, but there was no precise date of his birth. Accordingly, Justice Thompson arranged the possible dates of birth within a matrix of three different cases, where in each case Inglis' citizenship "followed the condition of his father" (*jus sanguines*) and where in two cases his citizenship was at the same time consistent with place of birth (*jus soli*). The matrix was as follows:

1. "If [Inglis] was born before the 4th of July 1776, he was born a British subject." Before the 4th was before the Revolution and thus New York was then a British colony. In these circumstances, place of birth, a British colony, and the "condition of his father" (British subjectship) are aligned so that the circumstances of Inglis' birth met both *jus soli* and *jus sanguines*.

2. But "If born after the 4th of July 1776, and before the 15th of September . . . when the British took possession of New York, his infancy incapacitated him from making any election for himself, and his election and character followed that of his father." His father was British; therefore, Inglis was born British though born on US soil. Thus, *jus sanguines* (his "character followed that of his father") determined citizenship.

3. And, "If born after the British took possession of New York, and before the evacuation [in] 1783, he was . . . born a British subject, under the protection of the British government." Again, the circumstances of his birth met both *jus soli* and *jus sanguines*.

common law declares that the individual cannot put off his allegiance by any act of his own." But again, this faithful-to-*Calvin's-Case* reasoning was that of a dissenter, not that of the majority of the Court.

If the Supreme Court's decisions in *Shanks v. Dupont* and *Inglis v. Trustees of Sailor's Snug Harbor* are subject to a doctrinal rating, they are more of a public law than a *Calvin's Case* school of thought. More accurately, though, these decisions are pragmatic rather than doctrinal, with fair results, fitness for citizenship, and appropriate national policy being the objects of that pragmatism. Accordingly, these opinions drew on sources consistent with those objects. In the penultimate sentence of *Shanks v. Dupont*, Justice Story described the various sources used in that case, saying that it was "sustained by principles of public law, as well as of the common law, and by the soundest rules of interpretation applicable to treaties between independent states."

A Massachusetts Supreme Court decision, of which Story in *Inglis v. Trustees of Sailor's Snug Harbor* was mindful, was similarly pragmatic. In *Kilham v. Ward*, the claimant had been born in Salem prior to the Revolutionary War, had departed Salem for Newfoundland in 1775 and just prior to the Revolution, and had returned to Salem in 1780. Years later, as he attempted to vote in a Salem election, his vote was contested because he was a not citizen. He had been born in Massachusetts before July 4, 1776 and thus born, it was said, a British subject. Furthermore, because he had not been in the United States in 1776 and by virtue of the Declaration of Independence subjectship into US citizenship, he could not claim US citizenship owing to that absence. In issue then was whether Kilham, having been born on then British soil and thus born a British subject, remained a British subject owing to the perpetual allegiance doctrine of *Calvin's Case*, which doctrine the court stated as follows:

> [E]very person born within a realm owes allegiance to the sovereign thereof, and this allegiance cannot be forfeited, cancelled, or changed, by any change of time, place, or circumstance. . . . And therefore, where two kingdoms are united under one sovereign, and afterwards separated, all persons born therein during the union owe allegiance to their first sovereign. . . . This doctrine is fully stated and approved in Calvin's case.

This statement of the doctrine was but to show that the court did not follow it. Rather than finding that Kilham was a British subject as prescribed by *Calvin's Case*, the court found that instead he was an American citizen. He was so owing not to place of birth but instead to considerations such as the Jay treaty that concluded the Revolutionary War, relevant state statutes, his domicile at Salem, and him assuming the duties of a citizen.[46] Of the *Kilham v. Ward* case, Justice Story's take in *Inglis v. Trustees of Sailor's Snug Harbor* was that it "appears to me ... rational and just, and founded upon ... a clear principle of reciprocity and public policy."

Notwithstanding the preceding cases, Supreme Court decisions and all, the antebellum period produced a single state court decision by a single judge, of New York's Chancery Court, that unqualifiedly found that the common law per *Calvin's Case* was the proper measure of citizenship in the United States. This case, *Lynch v. Clarke*, is the centerpiece to the claim that the territorial measure of *Calvin's Case* was the rule in antebellum America.[47] The fact, though, is that *Lynch v. Clarke* was later trumped by a unanimous decision of New York's highest court, in *Ludlam v. Ludlam*. This latter case turned on an affiliation with the United States as established by descent from citizen parents and found that citizenship "does not depend upon the boundaries of the place."

First *Lynch v. Clarke*: While the Act of 1790 provided birthright citizenship to all children of immigrants who were naturalized as US citizens, it did not do so for persons who might come to the United States, had a child during their time here, and then, without being naturalized as citizens, returned to their native land. Julia Lynch was such a child. Her parents had come to New York from Ireland, stayed for a while, and then went back to Ireland. In the words of the court, Julia's family had come here "as an experiment, without any settled intention of abandoning their native country" and "after trying the country, they returned to their native land." In the course of that try-out and a few months before her parents returned to Ireland, Julia was born in New York. She went to and remained in Ireland with them, there as a subject and resident and where she was when her Uncle Thomas died in New York. Thomas left a will under which Julia claimed she had been conveyed property in New York.

---

46. Kilham v. Ward, 2 Mass. 236 (1806). Regarding the treaty and as said by Justice Sedgwick, "The treaty, on the part of Great Britain, stipulates 'for and with the people,' the 'inhabitants,' the 'citizens' of the United States. By these several names are they called in the treaty. And it does seem to me that the facts disclosed show that he was, at the time of the treaty, one of the people, a citizen of the United States, and an inhabitant of Salem, there having his domicile." *id.* at 244. Similar considerations ran though the separate opinions of the other justices, as did factors such as Kilham's long time domicile and lawful business in Salem and his loyalty to our cause during the conflict with England.

47. Lynch v. Clarke, 1 Sand. Ch. 583 (N.Y. 1844).

Under New York law, only a citizen could inherent real property. Julia claimed that she was a citizen, was so under *Calvin's Case*. This claim was opposed, among other things on the grounds that *Calvin's Case* set a rule of subjectship rather than of citizenship, that by it the Crown captured for life subjects "to man her fleets and armies . . . and supply her workshops" and did so without regard to any "principle" of republican government. Otherwise, public law, as had been prescribed by Justice Story and Vattel, was argued as follows:

> It is permanent residence, with the intent of remaining, added to birth, which creates and establishes the political character. Without such *permanent residence,* and while the parent is *in itinere,* the place of birth follows the allegiance of the father. . . . It is the sensible doctrine of Vattel and of Story. . . . [W]as the father of Julia an alien? Was his visit here temporary? did he intend to return home, and did he in fact return home and die there, she *dwelling with him* at the time of his death? If so, her condition followed his, and she was a British subject.

None of which was convincing to the judge, Assistant Vice-Chancellor Sanford, who heard and decided the case. Although the Constitution did not define birthright citizenship, that document, Sanford noted, did refer to the "natural born citizen" as it defined the qualifications of the President. Sanford locked on to that phrase, "natural born" and asked, "Suppose a person should be elected president who was native born, but of alien parents, could there be any reasonable doubt that he was eligible under the Constitution?" His answer was "I think not," which seems a bit quick. Defining natural born by reference to *Calvin's Case* includes absurdities, such as a person born here to foreign nationals on vacation being eligible for the presidency while a person born to citizens overseas in service of this nation does not. Be that as it may, the vice-chancellor ruled that under *Calvin's Case* "Julia Lynch was a natural born citizen of the United States."

Nineteen years after *Lynch v. Clarke*, the New York Court of Appeals again took up the issue of the birthright citizenship, now by the full bench of the state's highest court. Unanimously, this court stood the conventional view of *Calvin's Case* on its head, saying that properly understood the case actually did not support place of birth as the measure of birthright citizenship. As said, this case was *Ludlam v. Ludlam*. In *Ludlam* as in *Lynch*, at issue was whether the claimant, Maximo Ludlam, was a US citizen and as such entitled to inherent real property in New York. The context was different in that Ludlam had not been born in the United States but instead had been born abroad, in Peru but to a US citizen. Although citizenship to children born abroad was widely available under Congress' 1790 Act for children "born beyond of the seas" to citizens, that Act did not, because of a certain warp, as previously noted, apply to Ludlam.[48]

Without a statute on point, the court decided Ludlam's claim to birthright citizenship as by reference to fundamental law, which was discerned by reference to various sources. Regarding English sources, the court started some 400 years before *Calvin's Case* and came to a different view of that case. The Court examined the Statute of 25 Edw. III, which provided that children born to English subjects while they were abroad ("beyond the seas") were born as subjects and born as such because of their "natural allegiance" to the Crown, meaning that their allegiance consisted of a disposition that followed that of their parents. With that, the court turned to *Calvin's Case* and turned it around: In the words of the court, birthright citizenship had been "very elaborately examined in *Calvin's case*" and that "among the principles settled in that case, and which have remained unquestioned since, are these. . . ."

Of these "principles settled", the first was that "That natural allegiance does not depend upon locality or place; that it is purely mental in its nature, and cannot, therefore, be confined within any certain boundaries; or, to use the language of Coke, that 'liegeance, and faith and truth, which are her members and parts, are qualities of the mind and soul of man, and cannot be circumscribed within the predicament of *ubi*" (*ubi* means territory). With *Calvin's Case* thus perceived, the court concluded that birthright citizenship "does not depend upon the boundaries of the place." Rather, it depended on a "natural allegiance" formed by human relations in general and familial relations in particular. As found by the court, citizenship "must be . . . transmitted from parents to the child or it could not exist." By this standard, Maximo Ludlam, having been born abroad to a US citizen, was born as a citizen.

Apart from the foregoing sources, the court relied on public law for its conclusion that the citizenship of the child followed that of the parents. Vattel was cited and followed. In the words of the court:

> [T]he doctrine that children . . . follow, in regard to their political rights and duties, the condition of their fathers, [is] founded in natural law, and to be substantially the same in most, if not all, civilized countries. Vattel says, "Society not being able to subsist and perpetuate itself but by the children of its citizens, those children naturally follow the condition of their fathers and *succeed to all their rights*. . . . The *place of birth* produces no change in this particular, and cannot of

---

48. The warp in coverage of the 1790 Act is described at pp. 54.

itself furnish any reason for taking from a child what *nature has given him.*

Otherwise, the court relied on the republican nature of American citizenship, noting that by it we had rejected the doctrine of "perpetual allegiance" that was the ineluctable and "inseparable" consequence of membership as determined by place of birth.[49]

*Lynch v. Clarke* is the only antebellum decision (and apparently the only case in our history) that squarely holds that *Calvin's Case* determines citizenship in the United States. And whatever light *Lynch v. Clarke* provides should be adjusted by the fact that it was the opinion of a single New York judge and that thereafter, in *Ludlam v. Ludlam*, that state's highest court with all justices concurring spoke differently, saying that birthright citizenship depended on birth within circumstances of affiliation with and loyalty to a nation and did not, as the court stated, "depend upon the boundaries of the place."

# The "Natural Born Citizen"

In 1787 as it does today, Article II of the Constitution requires that the President be a "natural born citizen."[50] The provision is that "No person except a natural born Citizen . . . shall be eligible to the Office of President." What those words might mean, as a one-place identifier of the citizen, then as now in 1787, is unclear. But we can guess from constitutional history and possibly a 1790 enactment of Congress.

But before going to these sources, a place to start is with a recent example — as provided by Sen. John McCain. In 2008, McCain was the Republican nominee for President. He had been born in Panama; his parents lived there in the course of military service. The question then asked, given that McCain was born in Panama, was whether he was a "natural born citizen." The question was unanswered.[51] But as said, there may be an answer by constitutional history as assisted by a 1790 congressional enactment.

---

49. Ludlam v. Ludlam, 26 N.Y. 356 (1863).

50. Article II provides: "No person except a natural born Citizen, or a Citizen of the United States, at the time of the Adoption of this Constitution, shall be eligible to the Office of President; neither shall any Person be eligible to that Office who shall not have attained to the Age of thirty-five Years, and been fourteen Years a Resident within the United States."

51. There was a lawsuit but no standing. Hollander v. Senator John McCain, 566 F.Supp.2d 63 (D. New Hampshire 2008).

The constitutional history is of a European royalty of princes who might insinuate themselves into power in America, with the presidency being the point of entry. John Jay, by a letter of July 25, 1787 to George Washington, said as much, "Permit me to hint whether it would not be wise and seasonable to provide a strong check to the admission of Foreigners into the administration of our national Government, and to declare expressly that the Commander in Chief of the American army shall not be given to nor devolve on, any but a natural *born* Citizen." For reason, then, of "a strong check to the admission of Foreigners into the administration of our national Government", the phrase "natural born citizen" became part of the Constitution.

The fear that underlay the "No person except a natural born citizen . . . shall . . . be President" is understandable. For instance, by a 1701 enactment England had left the door open for the ascension of European princes to the English throne and that opening had been used on three occasions by the German House of Hanover to gain control of England. On this side of the Atlantic, Mexico, without a constitutional wall against royalty, was infected by it, as Maximilian Ferdinand of the Royal House of Austria became Maximilian I of Mexico. That ascendancy led to civil war and Maximilian's execution in Mexico. Farfetched or not, our "natural born citizen" standard was part of a structure against royalty. Accordingly, St. George Tucker, writing in 1800, described the purpose of the standard as follows:

> That provision in the constitution which requires that the president shall be a native-born citizen . . . is a happy means of security against foreign influence. . . . [A] total exclusion from a station to which foreign nations have been accustomed to, attach ideas of sovereign power, sacredness of character, and hereditary right, is a measure of the most consummate policy and wisdom. . . . The title of king, prince, emperor, or czar . . . would have rendered him a member of the fraternity of crowned heads: their common cause has more than once threatened the desolation of Europe.

As a "natural born citizen" guards against a foreigner being President, it carries a worry. Does "natural born" mean birth on US soil or instead mean descent from a citizen? In 1787, when "natural born citizen" was added to the Constitution, perhaps we had no idea of how *naturally* to gain citizenship, whether by birth on our soil or by descent from a citizen. Just a few years later we did. By a process of reasoning we have covered, the original citizens were the "We the People" named by the Constitution. Thereafter, descendants of those people gained citizenship by birth to them. Shortly after the Constitution was enacted, then, we had a generally accepted method, birth from a citizen, of gaining citizens. The value of the measure, as said by Justice Story on the Supreme Court, is that it gained the citizenship of the child, as the child "partake[s] of the national character" of the parents. Or as said by Justice Fuller of the Court, "I submit that it is unreasonable to conclude that 'natural born citizen' applied to everybody born within the geographical tract known as the United States, irrespective of circumstances; and that the children of foreigners, happening to be born to them while passing through the country, whether of royal parentage or not,. . . were eligible to the presidency, while children of our citizens, born abroad, were not."[52]

By a fair reading of those Justices and from the practice, started soon after the Constitution was adopted, "natural born citizen" applies to persons born to citizens, regardless of the soil on which they were born. If that is the case, then John McCain, born of a citizen, was a "natural born citizen" as required by the Constitution. Moreover, that reading of "natural born citizen" is supported by a 1790 enactment of our first Congress, as provided that "the children of citizens . . . that may be born beyond the seas . . . shall be considered as natural born citizens." Consequently, John McCain born abroad, is again found to be a "natural born citizen." If we were to pick at the answer, we would start, maybe, with the whole enactment, which is:

[A]ny Alien being a free white person, who shall have resided within the limits and under the jurisdiction of the United States for the term

---

52. Tucker's account of the purposes of Article II's natural born citizen requirement is from St. George Tucker, *Blackstone's Commentaries: With Notes of Reference to the Constitution and Laws of the Federal Government of the United States; and of the Commonwealth of Virginia (Philadelphia, Birch and Small, 1803)*. Justice Story's reference to national character are from Inglis v. Trustees of Sailor's Snug Harbor, 28 U.S. at 99, 170 and Shanks v. Dupont, 28 U.S. at 242, 245. Justice Fuller's comments are in United States v. Wong Kim Ark, 169 U.S. at 649, 715. And to quote the source of those comments, Vattel, "it is necessary that a person be born of a father who is a citizen; for, if he is born there of a foreigner, it will be only the place of his birth, and not his country."

As a phrase and concept, "native born" is used to describe the place-of-birth notion of natural born citizen. However, for birthright citizenship "native" better refers to descent from persons from that country than to birth within its borders. We would not naturally refer to a person born in Russia to United States citizens there on vacation as a native born Russian. In its (old French) origins, native relates to birth in the sense of that which is innate. Innate better refers to the parents than to where one is born to them. Recall that at Athens, the polis was not the territory but rather the people, them referring to Athens as *hoi Athenaoi*, the body of citizens. The same can and has been said of us, as by Supreme Court saying that the "Nation's citizenry is the country and the country is its citizenry". Afroyim v. Rusk, 387 U.S. 253, 268 (1967).

of two years, may be admitted to become a citizen thereof on application to any common law Court of record in any one of the States wherein he shall have resided for the term of one year at least, and making proof to the satisfaction of such Court that he is a person of good character, and taking the oath or affirmation prescribed by law to support the Constitution of the United States, . . . such person shall be considered as a Citizen of the United States. And the children of such person so naturalized, dwelling within the United States, being under the age of twenty one years at the time of such naturalization, shall also be considered as citizens of the United States. And the children of citizens of the United States that may be born beyond Sea, or out of the limits of the United States, shall be considered as natural born Citizens.[53]The enactment combined naturalization with the separate measure of born abroad to a citizen. Naturalization produced a "citizen" but not a citizen who can be President. Birth abroad to a citizen, though, gained a "natural born citizen." Surely, the first Congress, which was in place as the Constitution was adopted, understood that the "natural born citizen" could be President. Altogether, the constitutional history as assisted by the 1790 enactment altogether shows that Senator McCain, albeit born in Panama, was a natural born citizen.

---

53. 1 Stat. 103 (1790).

# Chapter Five

# Birthright Citizenship and the Fourteenth Amendment

"All persons born or naturalized in the United States, and subject
to the jurisdiction thereof, are citizens of the United States and of
the state wherein they reside."

For the United States, the founding generation was the original citizens. As
a matter of course, albeit a course not specified by legal text, that generation
transmitted its citizenship to their descendants. Moreover, the United States
welcomed immigration, and in this context legal text was not silent. The First
Congress in its first session provided citizenship by way of immigration. By
oath and after a period of residency in the United States, immigrants might
be naturalized as citizens. By that same act children of these immigrants
became citizens as their parents were naturalized. If their parents died before
completing the course of naturalization, their children received citizenship
in that case too. Birthright Citizenship was to an extent available for Native
Americans if they chose to live among us and outside tribal government and
if provided by treatises between tribal and federal governments.

However well citizenship may have worked for others in the years before
the Civil War, it worked not at all for African Americans. They were wholly
excluded from citizenship, which was sealed by the Supreme Court's decision in *Dred Scott v. Sandford*, where the Supreme Court had wrapped
itself in constitutional law and pronounced that persons of African descent
never had been or never could be citizens, either by birth or by naturalization.[54] Initially, *Dred Scott v. Sandford* had a certain positive reception.
While that decision was pending, the Democratic candidate and later

---

54. Dred Scott v. Sandford, 60 U.S. 393 (1856).

President James Buchanan pronounced that the matter of black citizenship "will be speedily and finally settled" and to the Court's decision "in common with all good citizens, I shall cheerfully submit." The decision when rendered settled nothing. Quite the contrary, as famously stated by Rep. James Wilson, republican of Iowa and an active participant in the ensuing struggle for civil rights for African Americans, "The opinion of the court was soon after given to the country, but instead of becoming a triumphant platform for the Democratic party, it proved to be the scaffold on which the party was executed."

After the ensuing war, *Dred Scott v. Sandford* was overturned and African Americans were made citizens by the nation as a whole, by amending the Constitution through the Fourteenth Amendment. Setting the measure by which African Americans could best be made citizens was not easy. Descent from citizen parents would not work so well in that under the *Dred Scott* case black parents were not citizens. What might more readily work was place of birth: The African Americans would become citizens if born here. During the Civil War and when asked how a black man might be a citizen, Attorney General Bates did not exactly jump to an answer. In his words, "I have often been pained by the fruitless search in our law books and the records of our courts, for a clear and satisfactory definition of the phrase citizen of the United States. I find no such definition.... [T]he subject is now as little understood ... as it was at the beginning of the Government." But while Bates found the relevant sources confusing, he still posited a basis of citizenship, which was birth on US soil. However, and as he apparently knew—Bates referred to the "accident of birth"—location of birth did not necessarily establish a meaningful connection with the nation, as should be the norm for citizens.[55]

Bates' opinion resolved nothing. Work of that magnitude would have to be done by the nation at large. Accordingly, after the war and in the weeks before debate began in Congress on African American citizenship, a leading abolitionist publication, the *National Anti-Slavery Standard,* proposed a constitutional amendment as the medium of change. The proposed amendment included place of birth as a measure of citizenship. At the same time, though, the measure was qualified by a requirement of connection with the nation. This connection was that of permanent residency, of being lawfully settled among us. The proposal was that "No State shall make any distinction in civil rights and privileges among ... among persons born on its

---

55. 10 U.S. Op. Atty. Gen. 382 (1862). An African American had sought a license as a river boat pilot, for which he had to be a citizen and Bates opined that he was.

soil of parents permanently resident there, on account of race, color, or descent."[56]

Connection as shown by "parents permanently resident" had by then been verified by history. In 1790, Congress provided that "the children of citizens . . . that may be born beyond the seas . . . shall be considered as natural born citizens," but then it qualified the measure with a qualifier of residency, stated as "the right of citizenship shall not descend to persons whose fathers have never been resident in the United States." This qualifier was added so as to avoid awarding birthright citizenship to parents who otherwise might have no connection with the nation and might "evade the duties and responsibilities of American citizenship." The relation of a permanent legal residency (or domicile) to citizenship was thereafter amply recognized by Justice Story as he noted "the great question . . . respecting the effect of domicile on national character forms the leading point in many cases before the Court." Also from the Supreme Court bench, Justice Bushrod Washington (George Washington's nephew) distinguished the civil status of "those who reside there from a permanent cause" from others with only a transient relation with the nation. In this respect, Washington referred to and relied on public law as follows:

> The writers upon the law of nations distinguish between a temporary residence in a foreign country, for a special purpose, and a residence accompanied with an intention to make it a permanent place of abode. The latter is styled by Vattel, domicile, which he defines to be, "a habitation fixed in any place, with an intention of always staying there." Such a person, says this author, becomes a member of the new society.[57]

African Americans were permanently, deeply, and lawfully rooted in our society and thus rightfully were members. Domicile was a way of capturing that rightfulness. Accordingly, the *Anti-Slavery Standard* proposed birthright citizenship for persons "born on its soil of parents permanently resident there."

The significance of the relation, of "born on its soil of parents permanently resident there," should not be missed. As the Fourteenth Amendment later defined birthright citizenship, it included and required a

---

56. The proposal was first published in the *New Orleans Tribune* on December 24, 1865 and later published in the *National Anti-Slavery Standard* on February 24, 1866. This latter publication coincided with the commencement of congressional debate on birthright citizenship, and then in connection with the Civil Rights Act of 1866.

57. The Venus, 8 Cranch 253, 277–78 (1814).

relation with the nation but stated that relation abstractly, as "subject to the jurisdiction." That abstraction has included the "parents permanently resident there" fact of the *Anti-Slavery Standard* proposal, which is shown, indeed held to be a case, in two of the three cases in our history that deal with birthright citizenship under the Fourteenth Amendment. In these cases, birthright citizenship turned on domicile, on "the general rule," as said in *Benny v. O'Brien*, that "when the parents are domiciled here, birth establishes the right to citizenship."[58]

Moreover, the predecessor of the Fourteenth Amendment, the historic Civil Rights Act of 1866, included African Americans in our civil society by means of an inclusive definition of birthright citizenship. Same as the *Anti-Slavery Standard*, birthright citizenship under this act was triggered by domicile. In the letter that presented the Act to the President for his signature, the Act's author and mover, Sen. Lyman Trumbull, wrote, "The Bill declares 'all persons' born of parents domiciled in the United States, except untaxed Indians, to be citizens of the United States."[59] Today, the various bills introduced in Congress that would define birthright citizenship uniformly include domicile as part of the definition. Same as William Faulkner said in *Requiem for a Nun*, "The past is never dead. It's not even past."

# "Rights of Citizens": The Civil Rights Act of 1866

African Americans first came to North American in 1621, at Jamestown when a Portuguese ship unloaded twenty-one people they purchased from West African tribes. At that time these people were thought of as indentured. But shortly that status changed, to slavery. For them there was no Ellis Island.

Not slavery — it took the civil war to end that practice — but the importation of slavery ended in 1808. As the Constitution was debated in 1787, three states threatened to leave the convention if importation of slaves was banned. The compromise reached was set out in Article I of the Constitution that "The Migration or Importation of such Persons as any of the States now existing shall think proper to admit, shall not be prohibited by the Congress prior to the Year one thousand eight hundred and eight." (Also, that provision was a roundabout way of not admitting the practice of slavery.)

---

58. Benny v. O'Brien, 58 N. J. Law, 36, 40, 32 Atl. 696 (1895).

59. The Trumbull letter was uncovered and reported by Mark Shawhan, The Significance of Domicile in Lyman Trumbull's Conception of Citizenship, 119 Yale L. J. 1351 (2010).

In 1808, Congress acted to prevent the importation of slaves, by providing that no one could "import or bring into the United States or the territories thereof from any foreign kingdom, place, or country, any negro, mulatto, or person of colour, with intent to hold, sell, or dispose of such [person] . . . as a slave." (The congressional act now said "slave".)

The importation of slaves was prohibited but slavery was not. In the South, about four million persons were slaves in 1860. Above the Mason Dixie, most states did not allow slavery, but in those states and in the nation as a whole, African Americans were not citizens. The civil war ended slavery and after the war the whole nation made African Americans citizens.

When the Citizenship Clause of the Fourteenth Amendment was introduced in Congress, it came with the statement that "the question of citizenship has been so fully discussed in this body as not to need any further elucidation." Indeed, "the question" had been extensively debated — and debated seems too mild a word, bitterly disputed and dissected seem better — in a legislative conflict that had stretched from January 29 to April 10, 1866 to about three weeks before debate began on the Clause. That preceding struggle had been about and resulted in a landmark piece of legislation, the Civil Rights Act of 1866. Considering that the Fourteenth Amendment, coming on the heels and momentum of that Act, was meant to infuse "citizenship and the rights of citizens" as declared by the 1886 Act into the Constitution, careful consideration of the Act is essential.[60]

African Americans had then emerged from slavery, but not necessarily into the same civil liberty as enjoyed by the rest of the nation. This liberty included the chance to work, contract, hold property, share public goods, and participate in our society and economy. The aim of the Civil Rights Act was to assure that liberty for African Americans. For this book, the cogent question is how did the Act propose to do that? The answer is that in a rather evolutionary process, a progression through Congress shaped by opposition, the Act came to embed these civil liberties in status of the citizen and opened that status to African Americans by means of birthright citizenship.

In large part, this move toward birthright citizenship was at the direction of a perhaps under-unappreciated statesman, Sen. Lyman Trumbull, a Republican from Illinois. Trumbull was a person of intellect braced

---

60. Deliberations about and references to the Civil Rights Act and then to the Fourteenth Amendment as presented in this chapter are from the Congressional Globe as it presents debates and proceedings in the first session of the Thirty-Ninth Congress. The debates on the Civil Rights Act I refer to are from January 29, 1866 to April 10, 1866. For the most part I will omit specific references to the Globe.

by integrity. He had been born in Colchester, Connecticut, educated at the Bacon Academy, commenced teaching at age sixteen, and was a headmaster four years later. He then read and entered a career in law, in Illinois where he had moved and served on the state's highest court before he entered the US Senate. In politics, Trumbull started as a Democrat but then left that party because of its support for slavery. In the Republican Party, he was no hack. For example, notwithstanding his stalwart opposition to President Andrew Johnson on the matter of civil rights, he was one of the three Republican Senators to vote against his impeachment. By Trumbull's lights, the impeachment process had been factional, procedurally deficient, and unfair. In the Senate, Trumbull had co-authored the constitutional provision, the Thirteenth Amendment, which ended slavery, and helped secured its passage from his post as chairmen of the Senate Judiciary Committee. Although that Amendment ended slavery, it did not, as Trumbull said, make African Americans fully "independent." In a long speech in the Senate, Trumbull declared that in itself the black man's emergence from slavery "did not allow him to own property," "did not allow him to enforce his rights," and "did not allow him to be educated." Toward those ends, Trumbull said, "there is another bill on our table." That bill was the Civil Rights Act.

When first introduced by Trumbull, the bill (Senate Bill 61) that became the Act did not refer to citizenship. Instead, it referred to "inhabitants" (as had the Continental Congress before it), and provided that "There shall be no discrimination in civil rights or immunities among the inhabitants of any State or Territory of the United States on account of race, color, or previous condition of slavery." The rights instantiated in the bill were "to make and enforce contracts," "to hold, and convey real and personal property," and the "full and equal benefit of all laws and proceedings for the security of person and property."

African American participation in these goods was at first explained, by Trumbull, as being part of and required by the Thirteenth Amendment's abolishment of slavery. Immediately, that basis was assailed. The Amendment did indeed end slavery, as it was said, but just that and only that. In the words of a Democrat from Maryland, Senator Saulsbury, the Amendment provided only "that the *status* of slavery in this country shall not longer exist" and "has not said that Congress may exercise power in reference to anything else." Thus, the attempt "to confer civil rights which are wholly distinct and unconnected with the status or condition of slavery" was outside Congress's power. Although Trumbull had read the Thirteenth Amendment more broadly, he quickly came forward with a revision of the civil rights bill, which provided a wholly different basis, a basis apart from the Thirteenth Amendment, for the protection of civil liberties.

*This basis was citizenship.* The revision that Trumbull offered was to add a new first sentence, which was "That all persons of African descent born in the United States are hereby declared to be citizens of the United States." As African Americans were citizens, Trumbull explained, "Then they will be entitled to the rights of citizens, and what are they? The great fundamental rights set forth in this bill: the right to acquire property, the right to go and come at pleasure, the right to enforce rights in the courts, to make contracts, and to inherit and dispose of property."

But as soon as Trumbull moved to anchor the civil rights of African Americans in citizenship, that move was questioned. He was asked, "Where is the authority of Congress to make them citizens?" The immediate answer, by Trumbull, was naturalization, him saying that "The Constitution of the United States confers upon Congress the right to provide uniform rules of naturalization." Just as quickly, naturalization was disputed, first of all on *Dred Scott v. Sandford* grounds. Under constitutional law as declared in that case, the barrier against African American citizenship was sweeping and absolute: They had never been citizens, could not be born as citizens, and could not be naturalized as citizens. In words that carried forward *Dred Scott v. Sandford*, the claim, as made by Senator Davis of Kentucky, was that African Americans "most certainly were not counted among 'We the People'" that founded the nation and thus their descendants could not be made citizens, not by naturalization or by any kind of congressional enactment. A more technical objection was that as defined by practice naturalization was appropriately used for providing citizenship to persons from abroad and not for resolving domestic matters of citizenship.[61]

Moreover, the thought that naturalization was not quite the right process was shared by proponents of civil liberties for blacks. Rather than conferring citizenship by what seemed something of a finesse by naturalization, these Senators favored direct action, by Congress itself declaring and defining citizenship and doing so as a matter of fundamental law. And now and in opposition to *Dred Scott v. Sandford*, declaring that law correctly. As explained by Senator Morrill, a republican from Maine, if the Supreme Court could declare — as it had on some questionable history in *Dred Scott v. Sandford* — that blacks could not be citizens, Congress could and should

---

61. Senator Davis of Kentucky, one of the more formidable opponents of bill, cited commentaries and understandings, showing that naturalization was "the act of investing an alien" with citizenship. Twenty-six years later the Supreme Court showed the same sense, saying "Naturalization is the act of adopting a foreigner, and clothing him with the privileges of a native citizen." Boyd v. State of Nebraska, 143 U.S. 135, 162 (1892). African Americans were not aliens and thus they could not be naturalized, or so the argument went on.

declare otherwise, now based on good history and a sound appreciation of the "fundamental principle[s]" of "nature and nations." The better case, as put by Morrill, was that for citizenship, the bill should be "an affirmative proposition," a "declaration of a grand fundamental principle . . . of law and nations."

Thus explained, as a matter of fundamental law properly understood, birthright citizenship was at once a moral force, a key to civil society, and a means of civil rights. Although Trumbull the lawyer understood the technical possibilities of naturalization, Trumbull the statesman appreciated the moral force of a grand declaration of birthright citizenship. Moreover, at about that time the opposition made a challenge that Trumbull could not ignore. After offering *Dred-Scott* arguments that African Americans could not be made citizens, Senator Van Winkle closed his remarks by tossing a question in the direction of Trumbull. Van Winkle asked whether the people of America really wanted to open citizenship to African Americans, and also to "the races on the Pacific Coast," that is, the Chinese. "I would like," Van Winkle said, "to see . . . whether they are willing that these pie-bald races . . . be citizens with them in this country."

Trumbull had a response in hand. Throughout the debates Trumbull had moved swiftly, so that at times, as one reads and tries to understand the deliberations, effect seems to precede cause. Of that speed and as said by Senator Van Winkle: "I am speaking without immediate preparation. I did not suppose that this subject would have come before us as soon as yesterday." As soon as Van Winkle was seated, Trumbull rose to offer a new proposal respecting birthright citizenship. Trumbull's first proposal had been limited to "persons of African descent"; it had been "That all persons of African descent born in the United States are hereby declared to be citizens of the United States." Now he offered a more inclusive revision, remarkable because it was to become the substance of the Citizenship Clause of the Fourteenth Amendment. This revision defined, as Trumbull said, the "natural born citizen" and did so in the multicolored way that Van Winkle had declaimed. Rather than "persons of African descent," the revision applied across the board, to everybody, to "all persons. The terms now offered by Trumbull were that "All persons born in the United States, and not subject to any foreign power, are hereby declared to be citizens of the United States, without distinction of color." By these terms of "all persons" and "without distinction of color," citizenship was opened to all races, even those "on the Pacific Coast" included.

The incidental but yet important point — the point not just for citizenship but also for constitutional law in general, which I will now repeat — is that this new definition of birthright citizenship was conceived as a declaration, now by Congress, of a new fundamental law respecting citizenship. ("Declaration" is how the Act refers to itself; the Act says "declared.") As such, the Civil Rights Act was neither an exercise of Congress's power to enforce the Thirteenth Amendment respecting slavery nor an exercise by Congress of its power respecting naturalization. Although those bases of power were proposed as the Act evolved through Congress, neither basis (the Thirteenth Amendment or naturalization) included the power to define citizenship for the entire nation as the Act now did. Consequently, the Act was based on neither. The Act was, as said, a declaration of fundamental law (a "declaration of a grand fundamental principle,") as Senator Merrill said, respecting citizenship and civil liberties that attach to it. Given that the substance of the Act remains with us today, its grounding in the status of the citizen is today important.[62]

Past Congress' work to this point, directed to overcoming *Dred Scott v. Sandford* and anchoring civil liberties in birthright citizenship, there remained a hard issue the hard task of better defining that citizenship.

---

62. The problem of state of action (or said better a misconception of state action) in relation to civil liberties seems an instance of troubles caused by ignoring the grounding of civil liberties in the citizen. As protection of these liberties is based on the equal protection and due process clauses of the Fourteenth Amendment, the protection is only against state action, that is, actions by state or federal government. (By its terms, the Amendment requires state action in the cases of equal protection and due process.) These liberties are not thereby protected against private action, as where a privately owned hotel refuses to provide rooms to African Americans, a restaurant refuses to serve them, or a private school refuses to accept their kids. A solution to this state action problem has been to ground protection of civil liberties in constitutional provisions, such as the Commerce Clause (for the Civil Rights Act of 1964, *see* The Civil Rights Cases, 109 U.S. 3 (1883); Heart of Atlanta Motel v. United States, 379 U.S. 241 (1964)) and the Thirteenth Amendment (for 18 U.S. C. Sections 1981, 1982, & 1983, *see* Jones v. Alfred H. Mayer Co., 392 U.S. 409 (1986)), that do not require state action. As these bases may have been sufficient, they are neither necessarily essential nor as capacious as desirable, nor altogether historically correct. Respecting history, the 1866 Civil Rights Act as it grounded civil liberties in the status of a citizen did not require state action, so that a denial of jobs and such by private action was not outside the reach of federal law. As the Fourteenth Amendment then incorporated the principles of that act, it may be taken as including private actions that diminish the civil liberties that attach to citizenship. The phrase "attrition of parliamentary processes" starts to capture how things go awry as the status-of-the-citizen basis of the Fourteenth Amendment is missed. *See* Michael Anthony Lawrence, Rescuing the Fourteenth Amendment: How Attrition of Parliamentary Processes Begat Accidental Ambiguity; How Ambiguity Begat Slaughter House, 18 *William & Mary Bill of Rights* J. 445 (2009).

"Born of in the United States" by itself failed to require commitment to and affiliation with the nation. We were not a kingdom simply bent on acquiring subjects as had been England when it hatched a place of birth standard of subjectship. Instead, we were a republic where allegiance, affiliation, and incorporation into our communities all counted. Presence within the United States at the time of birth was by itself no assurance of those connections. For the most part, this fact was so palpable. Still, at times it was, as Representative Wilson, chairmen of the House Judiciary Committee, suggested that "persons born on our soil to temporary sojourners" should not receive birthright citizenship.[63] Or as in the several explanations, by Trumbull and others, that whether born here or not those who were of a less than full allegiance to the nation and its people were not eligible for birthright citizenship.

Respecting allegiance and in the terms of the bill as it had evolved, birthright citizenship was not open to persons who remained "subject to any foreign power." "Not subject to any foreign power," Senator Trumbull explained, meant "owing no allegiance to any foreign power." Moreover, this stipulation of undivided allegiance worked well for civil rights. As it excluded persons of insufficient connection, it included African Americans. They had been here and among us from the beginning and were not by anyone's imagination subject to some other power. As said in Congress, "All black persons born in the United States, who are not subject to any foreign power, would become citizens by virtue of birth."

Matters of affiliation and allegiance were further vetted in the context of a particular issue then at hand. As soon as Senator Trumbull offered the "All persons born in the United States and not subject to any foreign power" standard of citizenship, the question raised was: *How does it apply to Native Americans?* After considerable debate, there was a consensus answer, which was to adopt what was understood as prevailing practice. This answer as provided by Trumbull was that "They are already citizens of the United States if they are separated from their tribes and incorporated in your communities." As Native Americans chose to leave their tribes and to live among us, they showed an allegiance, affiliation, and assumption of the responsibilities of citizens sufficient for birthright citizenship. Accordingly, that citizenship was available to them. On the other hand, if they chose to

---

63. His words were: "We must depend on the general law relating to subjects and citizens recognized by all nations for a definition, and that must lead us to the conclusion that every person born in the United States is a natural-born citizen of such States, except . . . children born on our soil to temporary sojourners." His reference to "the general law . . . recognized by all nations" was surely a reference to public law rather than the common law per *Calvin's Case.*

live under tribal government that choice showed an allegiance to that government and for that reason they did not gain US citizenship.

Making this distinction between those Native Americans who left tribal government and those who had not was one thing. Expressing it was another. The fact and extent of tribal as opposed to federal and state governance was not always clear. Nor was it always clear whether Native Americans had so separated from tribal government as to be "incorporated in your communities." Given these difficulties of distinction, a long debate ensued, the not altogether satisfactory outcome of which was to add "Indians not taxed" to the bill, with that phrase serving as proxy for Native Americans insufficiently affiliated with the United States. This "Indians not taxed" phrase was offered by Trumbull, who said that "perhaps" it "would meet the views of all the gentlemen." His hope was that out of custom and usage, the terms "Indians not taxed" sufficiently distinguished those Native Americans who had assumed the responsibilities of citizenship from those who had not. In his words "Indians not taxed" was "a term used to designate those Indians . . . not counted as part of our people."

Thus amended, the civil rights bill provided citizenship as of right to "All persons born in the United States and not subject to any foreign power, excluding Indians not taxed." In final form, the bill provided that

> All persons born in the United States and not subject to any foreign power, excluding Indians not taxed, are hereby declared to be citizens of the United States, and such citizen of every race and color shall have the same right in every state and territory of the United States to the full and equal benefit of all laws and proceedings for the security of persons and property as is enjoyed by white citizens.

After more hard fights that included overcoming a presidential veto, this bill and its declaration of birthright citizenship became the Civil Rights Act of 1866.[64] Upon the final vote on April 10, the Congressional Globe pauses to note that the Speaker of the House's announcement that the bill had "become the law" and was "received with an outburst of applause, in which members of the House, as well as the throng of spectators, heartily joined, and which did not subside for some moments."

The purpose of the landmark Act was to secure for African American the benefits of our society. The means chosen was citizenship. Accordingly, as the Act moved through Congress, the headings under which the debates are recorded in the Congressional Globe changed from the "Civil Rights Act" to "Rights of Citizens." I have emphasized the Civil Rights Act of 1866

---

64. 14 Stat. 27, April 9, 1866.

as it provided for birthright citizenship. Not to be missed, though, is that the Act's egalitarian measure of citizenship was a dramatic movement and the movers knew it. As said on the floor of the Senate, "There is no parallel . . . in the history of any country. . . . The ancient republics . . . all had excepted classes." Consequently, Senator Morrill, who made that remark, pleaded guilty on the count that the equality part of the Act was a bit more than declaratory, that in fact it was "revolutionary." "I admit this species of legislation is absolutely revolutionary," he said, "But are we not in the midst of revolution? Is the Senator from Kentucky [Davis] utterly oblivious to the grand results of four years of war?"

## The Fourteenth Amendment

The very day the Civil Rights Act was celebrated in the House — with a sustained "outburst of applause" that "did not subside for some moments" — was the day the work began on infusing the Act into the written Constitution. On April 10, 1866, the resolution that would become the Fourteenth Amendment was reported, out of the Joint Committee on Reconstruction and to the Senate, came with the explanation that the proposed amendment would elevate "citizenship and the rights of citizens . . . under the civil rights bill" into the written Constitution.

It might be and was asked, if "citizenship and the rights of citizens" had been covered by the Civil Rights Act, why duplicate that coverage through the Fourteenth Amendment? For good reason was the answer. Be it a declaration of fundamental law or not, the fact that the Civil Rights Act had been enacted by Congress meant it could be repealed by a future Congress. The specific concern was that the Democratic Party that had opposed the Act might soon become the majority party and then overturn the Act. Repeal by a simple majority of Congress, though, could be averted by embedding the Act in the Constitution. Accordingly, as questions were raised about the Amendment being the same as the Civil Rights Act so why bother, the response was, "We propose to make these principles permanent" by writing them into the Constitution.[65]

Placing birthright citizenship as declared by the Civil Rights Act into the text of the Constitution first of all required an overhaul of the proposal (H. Res. No. 127) submitted to the Senate for its approval as the Fourteenth Amendment. The proposal came out of the Joint Committee on

---

65. Cong. Globe, 39th Cong., 1st Sess. 2768–69 (1866).

Reconstruction, where it had been drafted by Rep. John Bingham. Somehow, the proposal drafted failed to provide citizenship to African Americans.[66] Indeed, it failed to provide for or to define citizenship at all. But in the Senate, among veterans of the just finished struggle over citizenship and the Civil Rights Act, that deficiency was cured.

The short-lived but instructive (and earlier noted) first move was by Senator Wade of Ohio. With the end of race-blind citizenship in mind, Wade proposed that the proposed Amendment be open with the provision that "No state shall make or enforce any law which shall abridge the privileges or immunities of persons born in the United States or naturalized by the laws thereof." The race-blind purpose — providing civil rights through citizenship to all persons born in the United States — of that proposal was fine. The fact immediately noticed, though, was that under the Wade proposal the unqualified fact of birth in the United States was alone sufficient for citizenship, and that was not so fine.

Immediately, it was cause for dissent. Senator Wade himself remarked that, "The Senator from Maine suggests to me, in an undertone, that persons may be born in the United States and yet not be citizens of the United States." Sen. William Pitt Fessenden, the Senator from Maine and chairman of the Joint Committee on Reconstruction, took the floor to show how. He showed by a particular question the deficiencies in Wade's proposal. The question was, "Suppose a person is born in here of parents from abroad temporarily in this country?" Stated differently, did Wade really want to make place of birth the single measure of birthright citizenship and thus to provide that citizenship to persons of no substantial affiliation with the country?[67]

Shortly after the Wade–Fessenden exchange, the Senate Republicans went into a four-day caucus, of which we have no record but out of which

---

66. In drafting the report, John Bingham, at least I think so, was mainly concerned with protecting corporations from state regulation. In any event the report was not about citizenship for African Americans. Historians have been at odds about Bingham and the Joint Committee; there are numerous articles. An example is Richard L. Aynes, On Misreading John Bingham and the Fourteenth Amendment, 103 *Yale L. J.* 57 (1993). There are several biographies. For my own edification, I have read much of the work and still think Bingham was concerned with corporations and the states.

67. This sort of objection had not been limited to the Senate: As said, Representative Wilson, chairman of the House Judiciary Committee, a month earlier and during debate on the Civil Rights Act, had noted that the "natural born citizen" did not include "children born on our soil to temporary sojourners."

came the provision that is today the first sentence of the Fourteenth Amendment and is as such the Citizenship Clause. Unlike Wade's proposal, and same as the Civil Rights Act, this provision required more than birth on US soil. Beyond and apart from birth within the United States, it required a substantial affiliation with the country, the affiliation being stated as "subject to the jurisdiction." As for Wade's unqualified place of birth proposal, he withdrew it as soon as the birth-plus-affiliation standard of birthright citizenship was introduced.

The new first sentence was presented to the whole Senate by Sen. Jacob Howard of Michigan, who had been an active participant in the Civil Rights Act debate on citizenship and who now acted as the floor manager for the Fourteenth Amendment. In that capacity, Howard moved that the sentence be added to the Amendments and as added it provided that "All persons born or naturalized in the United States and subject to the jurisdiction thereof, are citizens of the United States." As regards the "great object" at hand, equality by means of citizenship for African Americans, this sentence (same as the Civil Rights Act) met it by the inclusive opening of "all persons," the point of inclusion that was so manifest as not to require much discussion. To be sure, Senator Cowan of Pennsylvania, vociferously and as he had in debate on the Civil Rights Act, asked whether the Chinese would thus qualify for birthright citizenship. The answer of course was that which allowed no distinctions as to *any* race. As said by Senator Fessenden, "all persons of every . . . race born in the United States, and subject to their jurisdiction . . . are citizens."

## The Standard: "Subject to the Jurisdiction Thereof"

In constitutional law as elsewhere, specificity has it uses. At times, it is better to state a hard-edged requirement, a rule that owing to its particularity can readily be applied. For instance, better to provide, as the Constitution does, the rule that no one can be President "who shall not have attained to the Age of thirty-five years" than to provide a more open measure, a standard as we say such as the President must be reasonably mature. That open-endedness would have invited debilitating uncertainties about the eligibility of candidates for that office. The sometime advantages of rules notwithstanding, the case remains that at times hard-edged rules cannot sensibly be set. Here the point, as stated by Chief Justice of the Supreme Court John Marshall, is that "it is a *constitution we are expounding.*" Constitutions must endure through the ages as over time changes will come and those changes cannot often or in all cases be foreseen. Consequently, the way of constitutions, particularly ours, is often not to set rules, which may prove too brittle, but instead to provide a standard to put into place a provision supple enough to deal with changes as come. For instance, the United States Constitution, albeit greatly concerned with fair trial procedures, does not specify a set of procedural rules but more flexibly provides for "due process."

For citizenship, "subject to the jurisdiction" is such a standard. To be sure, the consensus that produced it included some specific understandings about citizenship, as in Native Americans who had chosen to "incorporate into your communities" were entitled to birthright citizenship and as in persons only "temporarily present" in the United States were not. And there were more general understandings, as the necessity of a "full and complete" allegiance. All such understandings were stated together as "subject to the jurisdiction." This standard so stated is no more and ought not to be less than any other of the Constitution's "majestic generalities," such as equal protection, due process, or freedom of speech. But it has been less. Past some initial applications, by the courts and the executive branch as we shall see in the next chapter, the "subject to the jurisdiction" standard has since been mostly overlooked. Today, though, "subject to the jurisdiction" cannot well remain unseen, not given the massive movement of people into the country in violation of immigration law and the question they bring of whether birthright citizenship is open to them.

When it comes to understanding "subject to the jurisdiction," a couple of points need to be made up front. One is about the referent of the standard, the fact that parents are that referent. Common sense, "right reason" as John Locke put it, so dictates, as do deliberations on the Fourteenth Amendment. As is manifest in the light of common sense and in debates in Congress, eligibility for birthright citizenship turns on qualities of allegiance, affiliation, and reciprocity (a fair return for services rendered) that pertain to the parents and not the child. For the child, social facts are about the family rather than civic relations and responsibilities. Otherwise, the purpose of gaining persons disposed to be good citizens is served in that the children of parents, of an allegiance to and affiliation with a nation, are likely to absorb their civic character. Accordingly, when Senator Trumbull in his communiqué to the President on the Civil Rights Act presented the essentials of birthright citizenship, he described them as the relation "of *parents*" to the nation.[68]

A second point is about the word *jurisdiction*. Jurisdiction is a protean concept, developing and varying over time and circumstances. Which movement can be troublesome? As said by the Supreme Court, "jurisdiction is a word of many, too many, meanings." Perhaps, but not so much

---

68. As noted earlier in Chapter 5, other instances of the assumption that subject to the jurisdiction refers to parents.

once the context of the word is considered. Jurisdiction might simply be thought of as power, as in whether a state has power over a person. More particularly, though, jurisdiction can be viewed as the relation between person and polity that makes an exercise of that power rightful. This relational context is spelled out in today's concept of "personal jurisdiction." Jurisdiction here refers to whether a person can rightfully be called before the courts of a state to account for his or her alleged wrongs. For this jurisdiction, the dominant measure is relational, whether a person has by activities within the state established a relation with it so that an assertion of jurisdiction is "fair." Accordingly, in *Washington v. International Shoe*, the Supreme Court explained that a purely "present within the territory" measure of personal jurisdiction had been supplanted by fairness, by whether an assertion of jurisdiction is supported by "traditional notions of fair play and substantial justice." By no means exactly as in personal jurisdiction but by all means of a similar sense of relation and fair play, jurisdiction is used in the Citizenship Clause of the Fourteenth Amendment. This sense goes back at least to Chancellor Kent's opinion in *Goodell v. Jackson*, where he found that William Sagoharase, born in the United States as a member of the Oneida Tribe, was not a citizen. In that case "mere territorial jurisdiction" was not the measure of citizenship. Instead, affiliation with the "body politic, or people of the state" was.[69]

These points in mind, what do we know about the relation — of parents to nation — that subject to the jurisdiction entails? In a sentence, *we can and should know it means that they all — parents and child — are in.* "All in" in terms of a full and enduring commitment to the venture that is the United States, adventure really if you remember the challenge set by Benjamin Franklin that ours is a republican "if you can keep it." We understand "all in" by reference to the context and terms of debate on the Fourteenth Amendment, to the public law (as opposed to *Calvin's Case*) terms of that debate, and by common sense as held by republican minds.

Understanding also starts with knowing that the Amendment incorporated the Civil Rights Act of 1866, including its principle of an undivided allegiance that the Act stated as "not subject to any foreign power." But as Fourteenth Amendment incorporated the Act, it did so by somewhat

---

69. Relating jurisdiction and fairness, *see* Washington v. International Shoe, 326 U.S 310, 316 (1945). After the enactment of the Fourteenth Amendment, affiliation of person and polity as the essence of subject to jurisdiction gained the approbation of the Supreme Court. In Elk v. Wilkins, 112 U.S. 94, 101–02 (1884), the Court explained that subject to the jurisdiction did not simply mean location of birth. Rather, for the United States it required persons "completely subject to their political jurisdiction and owing them direct and immediate allegiance."

different wording. Where the Civil Rights Act had qualified birthright citizenship by excluding those "not subject to any foreign power" and "Indians not taxed," the Clause more shortly stated a principle of inclusion that persons "subject to the jurisdiction" gain birthright citizenship. Inasmuch as "subject to the jurisdiction" came out of the off-the-record caucus of Senate republicans, we lack a step-by-step explication of this new wording such as we have for the terms of the Civil Rights Act. Still, reasons for the change, from "not subject to any foreign power, excluding Indians not taxed" to "subject to the jurisdiction," are apparent.

Regarding "Indians not taxed": Under the Civil Rights Act that phrase was meant to differentiate between Native Americans who lived among us and had thus joined the broader political community, and between those who had "incorporated" into our communities and those who remained under tribal government. The former were understood as sufficiently affiliated with nation and people so as to gain birthright citizenship, whereas the latter not. Although Congress wished to continue that same understanding by means of the Fourteenth Amendment, it was not at the same time happy with the terms with which that understanding had been expressed. Though he had proposed it, Trumbull for one had never been entirely happy with the phrase "Indians not taxed." As he knew, a proper affiliation with our polity rather than taxation was the right consideration for citizenship to Native Americans. Accordingly, the Senate now eliminated "Indians not taxed" and instead included the purpose of that phrase, of assuring a full commitment to and assimilation within the nation, in the statement of "subject to the jurisdiction." Under this more positive statement and as before, Native Americans who had left tribal government to live among as ordinary citizens were entitled to birthright citizenship. Native Americans who remained under tribal government were not; they were not subject to the jurisdiction. In the words of Senator Howard, "Indians borne within the limits of the United States, and who maintain their tribal relations, are not, in the sense of the amendment, borne subject to the jurisdiction of the United States." Or as the Supreme Court would later say of Native Americans under tribal government: Although born within the "territorial limits" of the United States, they were not "subject to the jurisdiction in any legitimate sense."[70] More positively, those who had "incorporated your communities" were.

As subject to the jurisdiction included Native Americans sufficiently affiliated with our civic society, it similarly generally included "all persons"

---

70. Elk v. Wilkins, 112 U.S. at 94. Senator Howard's remarks are at Cong. Globe, 39th Cong., 1st Sess, at 2893.

so connected and disallowed those who were not. This intended operation of subject to the jurisdiction is shown by general principles of allegiance and commitment as stated throughout the debate and more specifically shown as Congress dealt with issues as it could then see or foresee. Congress then did see the problem of birthright citizenship, "parents from abroad temporarily in this country," it then did see the problem, as I shall shortly discuss, of parents partially as opposed to fully subject to our laws. It understood that in these instances the overriding consideration was a full and undivided allegiance and commitment to the United States. When Senator Fessenden was asked about the meaning of "subject to the jurisdiction of the United States" out of respect, he deferred that question to Senator Trumbull. Trumbull's answer was that "It means subject to the complete jurisdiction thereof. Not owing allegiance to anybody else. This is what it means."[71] Allegiance included law abidingness, a part more assumed than stated. Still it was, as by Representative Lawrence of Ohio, who noted that "citizen . . . imposes the duty of allegiance and obedience to the laws."

Apart from formal measures of allegiance, "subject to the jurisdiction" was explained, in fact more fully, in terms of a practical commitment to our civil society, a commitment of the sort that is characteristic of citizens. In the words of Senator Howard, the "subject to the jurisdiction" proviso "ought to be construed so as to imply a full and complete jurisdiction . . . that is to say, the same jurisdiction in extent and quality as applies to every citizen of the of the United States now." A relation that is in "extent and quality" the same as that of "every citizen of the United States" surely includes participation, contribution, and services in the manner of citizens. Same at the inception of democracy at Athens, citizenship was not to be gained simply by occupying space nor was birthright citizenship to be gained simply by being in a particular space.

## Neither a Synecdoche nor a Circumlocution

Today, the "subject to the jurisdiction" condition to birthright citizenship is often denied and done so by reading the Amendment in the manner of synecdoche, by viewing a part of a thing as the whole of a thing. By this view, birth in the United States is seen as the entire first sentence of the Amendment and its "subject to the jurisdiction" condition simply disregarded. For instance and as earlier noted about maternity tourism, the "born in United States" part of the Amendment omits the accompanying

---

71. Senator Trumbull's response when asked during drafting of the 14th Amendment, whether Native Americans would be covered by the Amendment.

"subject to the jurisdiction" qualifier and thereby concludes that birth on US soil by itself suffices for citizenship.

As do a number of scholars. These scholars, however, do not at the same time overlook the "subject to the jurisdiction." They understand that the Citizenship Clause is part of the Constitution and subject to the canon that no part of the Clause can be ignored. But at the same time, they substitute a tautology for the synecdoche. The tautology is that birth within the United States, automatically, always, and of itself, makes one subject to the jurisdiction of the United States. Consequently, "subject to the jurisdiction" *effectively* means born within the United States; consequently, it reiterates as opposed to qualifying place of birth. To illustrate (as I have before) in a joint congressional hearing on "Societal and Legal Issue Surrounding Children Born in the United States to Illegal Alien Parents," Professor Neuman testified that because these births were on US soil, by that single measure, those births generated citizenship as a matter of constitutional right. In his testimony, Professor Neuman did not ignore the subject to the jurisdiction standard, but instead reduced it to a nullity. He did so by saying that "Clearly, deportable aliens are subject to the jurisdiction of the United States — that is what makes them deportable. . . ."[72] To translate a bit, Professor Neuman says the fact that a person is subject to deportation, as is the case with persons here unlawfully, means we have some quantum of jurisdiction. Jurisdiction is assumed to be a power, deportable persons are subject to that power, and thus they are subject to jurisdiction. All of which reduce "subject to the jurisdiction" to a nullity, as it is called on then Cheshire-cat like it disappears.

With some prescience, however, this particular nullification was foreseen in debate on the Amendment, where it was referred to as "partial jurisdiction" and as such differentiated from "subject to the jurisdiction." Partial jurisdiction is this: Compliance with some part of the law and power of a nation (as respecting traffic laws or laws against trespass or personal assault and the like) is understood as a fair condition of entry to any country. As people enter a nation, on business, tourism, or to visit friends, it provides them the protection of law. Compassion and a nation's interest in trade and tourism assure this protection. In return for this protection and as said by John Marshall, those in receipt of it owe a "temporary and local allegiance": While within the nation they must abide by such parts of its law that apply to them. As more fully explained by Marshall, "When private individuals of one

---

72. Societal and Legal Issue Surrounding Children Born in the United States to Illegal Alien Parents, Subcommittee on the Constitution, House Judiciary Committee, 105th Cong. 1st Sess., at 107 (1995).

nation spread themselves through another as business or caprice may direct . . . it would be obviously inconvenient and dangerous to society . . . if such individuals or merchants did not owe temporary and local allegiance, and were not amenable to the jurisdiction of the country."[73]

*This "temporary and local allegiance" was referred to as "partial jurisdiction" in debate on the Amendment and as such rejected as the basis of birthright citizenship.* That "jurisdiction," limited as it is, did not qualify. It did not amount to "the full and complete" jurisdiction required by the Amendment. As said in debates on the Amendment, any person within the United States is "entitled, to a certain extent, to the protection of the laws"; for example, "an assault and battery on him" was unlawful same as an assault on a citizen and in return that person is bound to obey our laws as they apply to him. In return that traveler was obliged to abide by our laws while in the country. But that relation was not coextensive with citizenship, as explained in the debates by Senator Williams, a republican from New Jersey: "In one sense, all persons born within the territorial limits of the United States are subject to the jurisdiction of the United States, but they are not subject to the jurisdiction of the United States in every sense. . . . I understand the words here, subject to the jurisdiction of the United States to mean fully and completely subject to the jurisdiction of the United States."

Partial jurisdiction does not entail the assumption of commitments of the "extent and quality" expected of citizens. It does not make one subject to military service or a full range of taxes, it is not a basis for treason and or other obligations of a citizen, and thus it is no basis for birthright citizenship. Accordingly, partial jurisdiction would be rejected by the Supreme Court as a basis for birthright citizenship. In *Elk v. Wilkins*, the Court declared that the "evident meaning" of subject to jurisdiction under the Fourteenth Amendment was "not merely subject in some respect or degree to the jurisdiction of the United States, but completely subject to their political jurisdiction, and owing them direct and immediate allegiance."[74]

---

73. Schooner Exchange v. McFaddon, 11 U.S. 116, 144 (1812).

74. Elk v Wilkins, 112 U.S. at 94, 102. Senator Williams' remarks are at Cong. Globe, 39th Cong, 1st Sess., at 2897. The distinction between the complete jurisdiction that qualified for birth citizenship under the Fourteenth Amendment and the partial distinction was also drawn in commentary of that time. *See* George D. Collins, Citizenship by Birth, 29 *Am. L. Rev.* 385 (1895). For modern commentary, *see* John C. Eastman, Born in the U.S.A.? Rethinking Birthright Citizenship in the Wake of 9/11, (Sept. 29, 2005), available at http://ssrn.com/abstract=905570

# Regarding *Calvin's Case*

The main claim to citizenship, for illegal immigrants, is that the Fourteenth Amendment simply incorporates *jus soli* per *Calvin's Case* and by that measure made place of birth on our single and exclusive measure of birthright citizenship. The main problem with that claim is that it is makes no sense. It is anomalous if not absurd to think that we reverted to a condition used by royalty used to acquire subjects as our means of gaining citizens; it is contrary to the terms (which require more than place of birth) of the Fourteenth Amendment; and it is against common sense (e.g., why should children born here, say to tourists, gain citizenship). Consequently, *Calvin's Case* was in name and principle missing in action in deliberations on the Fourteenth Amendment. It was missing because no one thought that way. The principles then expressed were neither of *Calvin's Case* nor a presumed alleged common law under it. When the Citizenship Clause was first introduced in Congress, it came with the explanation that as it provided for citizenship it did so by reference to "natural law and national law," which is a public law rather than a common law frame of reference. Otherwise, public law rather than common law provided both the sense and terms of the debate, and *Calvin's Case* if it could be noted at all was noted by its absence.[75]

Indeed, had place of birth by *Calvin's Case* been the measure, there would not have been the need for the whole debate on the Citizenship Clause. The issues then struggled with would have not been problematic. All would have been easily resolved by reference to place of birth as set by

---

75. The introductory public law terms of reference, by Senator Howard, are at note 76. As to the absence of reverences in the debates to *Calvin's Case*: Proving a negative is hard. Still, I did not see the references. Here is a small (and confused) reference that can be found. Representative Lawrence of Ohio spoke in favor of birthright citizenship as provided by the 1866 Civil Rights Act (citizenship that was not consistent with *Calvin's Case*). In the course of that dialogue, he referred to Lynch v. Clarke, which had followed *Calvin's Case*. Lawrence mainly did so to make a point about citizenship being determined by federal rather than state law. That dialogue, though, included this statement: "all children born here are citizens without regard to the political condition or allegiance of their parents." Which statement is consistent with *jus soli* per *Calvin's Case*. He based that statement, though, not on *Calvin's Case* but on 25 Edward III, St. 2. That ancient enactment, however, had provided birthright citizenship for children born abroad to English subjects. As such, the enactment was based on the affiliation of the parents with England and therefore was with "regard to the political condition or allegiance of their parents" 1832 3d col.

*Calvin's Case.* There would have been no need to insist on full allegiance, no need to mark the distinction between partial and full jurisdiction, no call to avoid birthright citizenship for persons transiently among us, no need to be concerned about persons not "fully incorporated into your communities," no need to assure commitments of the "extent and quality" expected of citizens, and no call to redress these concerns through the Amendment's "subject to the jurisdiction" standard.

## Immigrants and Aliens

When Senator Howard introduced the first sentence of the Amendment, he described those who were not "subject to the jurisdiction" and thus not eligible for birthright citizenship. The Amendment "will not include," he announced to the Senate, "persons born in the United States who are foreigners, aliens, who belong to the families of embassadors or foreign ministers accredited to the Government of the United States."[76] But apart from an (unproblematic) exclusion of embassy and consular personnel from birthright citizenship, Howard's statement of exclusion runs to "foreigners" and "aliens." As it was made, that statement generated neither discussion nor objection. But today it does, as the foreigners and aliens terms of it are taken as denying citizenship to illegal immigrants. However, if they are disqualified from birthright citizenship, it is not so much or at all because of that statement by Howard. Disqualification is instead their failures of allegiance and commitments as owed by citizens, all of which is discussed in Chapter VIII. Otherwise, there is a lesson to be gained in unpacking that single statement by Howard respecting foreigners and aliens, because it helps show how the Citizenship Clause applies to immigrants.

Of the three cases we have on birthright citizenship under the Fourteenth Amendment, two are about immigrants. Of the two, the most solidly reasoned is *Benny v. O'Brien.*[77] In this case, the New Jersey Supreme Court held that "Allan Benny is a citizen of the United States in virtue of

---

76. Fully stated, Senator Howard's explanation was that:
This amendment which I have offered is simply declaratory of what I regard as the law of the land already that every person born within the limits of the United States, and subject to their jurisdiction, is by virtue of natural law and national law a citizen of the United States. This will not, of course, include persons born in the United States who are foreigners, aliens, who belong to the families of embassadors or foreign ministers accredited to the Government of the United States, but will include every other class of persons.
77. Benny v. O'Brien 58 NJL 36 (1895).

his birth here of alien parents, who at the time of his birth were domiciled in this country." On the face of it, either Senator Howard (as he appears to say that the Citizenship Clause is a blanket denial of birthright citizenship to aliens) or the New Jersey Supreme Court in *Benny v. O'Brien* (as it held that "alien parents . . . domiciled in this country" gain it) got it wrong. But then, the face of things is obscured by the word "alien."

Alien is a word out of time and out of place. According to John Kim, *Aliens in Medieval Law, The Origins of Modern Citizenship*, it comes out of Old French and the feudalistic premises of *Calvin's Case*.[78] Within feudalism, the newly born was subject to a lien, consisting of the liege lord's proprietary interest in the child's lifelong labor. Thus, alien referred to a person out of place, within a particular fiefdom but not of it because that person was owned (subject to a lien) by the lord of another place. In *Calvin's Case*, the lien translates to permanent subjectship, the duty of "perpetual allegiance" assessed by that case. In the United States, open as we are to immigrants, alien is neither an attractive nor generally accurate word. (Accordingly, I think of the Chinese grandparents of my grandchildren as immigrants rather than aliens.)

Expatriation, the act of throwing off an old allegiance in favor of allegiance to a new nation, is particularly a part of American history. We welcomed it while the British did not and about it we fought two wars, the War of 1812 as well as the Revolutionary War. Furthermore, in an underappreciated move made at the same time the Fourteenth Amendment was ratified, Congress endorsed and linked expatriation and immigration. Congress declared that "expatriation is a natural and inherent right of all people" and did so in light of the fact that "this government has freely received emigrants from all nations, and invested them with the rights of citizenship." As declared, we were not a society of subjects and as such closed to aliens. We were instead citizens and as such open to immigrants and immigration. Unlike the old concept of aliens, immigrants are not forever bound to the nation they departed. Instead they might and did come here, leaving old allegiances behind and to be a part of this country. They were not likely going back over the ocean.[79] They were staying and becoming

---

78. In particular, *see* p. 178 & n. 5 of Kim's book. The OED places alien in Old French, saying it generally meant "belonging to another person, place, or family." Similarly, not exactly the same, but perhaps parallel origin, Latin offers the words *alienun* (another person's property) and *alienus* (of another place or belonging to another).

79. Here's one reason, an account of a voyage to America by Norwegians, during the time in which the Fourteenth Amendment was enacted: "On the Victoria sailing in 1861 there were many deaths, and a ships carpenter was busy building coffins for the many children who died. A passenger later told how sad it was to see the little

Americans. Accordingly, for immigrants the rational for birthright citizenship under the Fourteenth Amendment kindly applies, to offer them birthright citizenship. By lawfully settling among us, they assume a full and complete allegiance to this nation and commitments and responsibilities of an "extent and quality as applies to every citizen of the United States."

In *Benny v. O'Brien*, the parents although not yet naturalized fitted the bill I just described. They had lawfully immigrated, were living lawfully and permanently among us, had applied for naturalization, and from all that appeared met commitments and responsibilities as expected of citizens. Accordingly, the Court found them entitled to birthright citizenship and that their son to have been born as a citizen. This being the case, Senator Howard, as he referred to aliens to debates on the Fourteenth Amendment, cannot be taken as including immigrants, because aliens they are not.

Indeed, at the time Howard spoke Congress he had long been mindful of immigrants and the merit of awarding them birthright citizenship. It had done so by the 1790 Act that provided that upon naturalization of their parents, the children of immigrants as well became citizens and by an 1804 amendment to the Act that provided that the immigrant "should die without having completed his naturalization, his widow and his children should be considered citizens upon taking the oaths prescribed by law."[80] Shortly before that 1804 enactment, George Tucker had stated the underlying mindset, saying that an immigrant here "to become a citizen . . . seems to have acquired a *right,* of which no *subsequent* event can divest him, without violating the principles of political justice, as well as of moral obligation."[81]

Not about immigration proper but the question that now divides the nation, of going around Ellis Island rather than through it: The question was not at all addressed in debate on the Fourteenth Amendment. A massive disregard of immigration law as is now the case was not imagined. That

---

coffins out on the seas as they sailed away. On the *Heros* sailing in 1868, the father of a child that died took his food chest for the coffin. The child of a relative had also died, and the two little bodies were laid together and buried in the ocean. The Ske family sailing on the Refondo in 1867 lost 4 children from pneumonia in one week. There were a lot of deaths on that voyage." The Irish referred to the vessels that brought them as "coffin ships."

80. 2 stat. 292, 293, March 26, 1804. *See generally* Boyd v. Nebraska, 143 U.S. at 135, 177.

81. St. George Tucker, *Blackstone's Commentaries: With Notes of Reference to the Constitution and Laws of the Federal Government of the United States and of the Commonwealth of Virginia* (1803/1969), available at http://press-pubs.uchicago.edu.

being said, the context of and deliberations on the Fourteenth Amendment provide an understanding of the Amendment sufficient to address the issue of birthright citizenship for persons living here unlawfully and to do so clearly, outside of obfuscations such as partial jurisdiction. This understanding is applied in Chapter 9.

# Chapter Six

# The Amendment Applied

The fruitful years in terms of the meaning of birthright citizenship under the Fourteenth Amendment came on early, in the thirty years following the Amendment's ratification, when issues — respecting birthright citizenship for persons only temporarily present within the United States, for Native Americans, and for children born to immigrants — were worked out by the courts and the executive branch. That was the productive period. Afterward, the period from 1898 to the present has been not been useful.

## Transient Connections

As regards a transient presence, the issue addressed in State Department opinions is whether birth on US soil is by itself sufficient for citizenship. These early opinions show that birth on US soil to parents of no permanent affiliation with the country does not give rise to citizenship.

Shortly after the Civil War, Richard Greisser was born in Ohio to a "German subject" who stayed in the United States on a temporary basis. Shortly after his birth, Richard and his parent returned to Germany. Years later, Richard asked the State Department whether he was a US citizen by right of his birth on our soil. The answer, by Secretary of State Thomas Bayard, was no. Although Richard had been born in the United States he had been born to a German parent living in the United States on a temporary basis. Under "public law," he was, as the Secretary said, "at the time of his birth of the same nationality as his father." That public law while persuasive was not necessarily dispositive, but the Fourteenth Amendment was. Because of the transient circumstances of his birth, the Secretary found that Richard Greisser was not "subject to the jurisdiction of the United States" within the Amendment's meaning and thus was not "a citizen of the United States by birth."

A bit earlier, Secretary of State Frelinghuysen had reached a similar conclusion. In the circumstances of a person "born of Saxon parents temporally in the United States," the Secretary found the claim he had gained birthright citizenship was "untenable" in that it is a "condition of citizenship that the person be not subject to any foreign power." Otherwise, Justice Miller of US Supreme Court in his 1891 *Lectures on the Constitution of the United States* explained that a child born to "a stranger or traveler passing through, or temporarily residing in, this country" did not receive US citizenship because the child was "not subject to its jurisdiction."[82] Thereafter, in 1895 in *Benny v. O'Brien*, the court found that the "born in the United States and subject to the jurisdiction thereof" terms of the Amendment "concede that there may be instances in which the right to citizenship does not attach by reason of birth in this country." Among those excluded were persons "born in this country of foreign parents who are temporarily traveling here."

Other nations, England for instance, have in modern times amended their laws to preclude practices such as maternity tourism. In the United States, though, that practice was already marked as insufficient as such by the Fourteenth Amendment.

# Native Americans

The Supreme Court first spoke of birthright citizenship under the Fourteenth Amendment just four years after the Amendment was enacted. In the *Slaughter House Cases*, 83 U.S. 36 (1873), the Court held that certain economic interests were not among the "privileges and immunities" of citizenship protected by the Amendment. In the course of that opinion, the Court described the purpose and scope of the Amendment's Citizenship Clause. The Court more or less repeated what Senator Howard had said, in debate on the Fourteenth Amendment, about foreign nationals: The Amendment's "subject to the jurisdiction" requirement, the Court said, "was intended to exclude from its operation children of ministers, consuls" as well "citizens or subjects of foreign states born within the United States." That statement, though, may have been dicta.

---

82. Both State Department opinions are found at Francis Wharton, *A Digest of the International Law of the United States*, 399–401 (1887). Justice Miller's view on parents only temporarily present is found at Samuel F. Miller, *Lectures on the Constitution of the United States*, 279 (1891). Otherwise, Justice Story, in his commentary, had much earlier suggested was not available to parents here for "temporary purposes." Joseph Story, *Commentaries on the Conflict of Laws*, 28 (1834).

Two years later, in 1874, the Court produced a holding exactly on point, in its first decision on birthright citizenship under the Fourteenth Amendment. In *Elk v. Wilkins*, a question was whether "merely by reason of his birth within the United States" that person gained citizenship under the Amendment. The Court's answer, among other things flatly inconsistent with *Calvin's Case*, what that the person did not, "merely by reason" of place of birth gain citizenship. The case had been brought by John Elk, a Native American born in the United States but within and under tribal government. The case thus involved the distinction, considered at length in debates on the Civil Rights Act and the Fourteenth Amendment, between those Native Americans who lived among us and had assumed the responsibilities of citizens and gained birthright citizenship and those who remained under tribal government and did not receive that citizenship. Because Elk's parents were among the latter group, the Court held that he had not been born as a citizen.

Elk argued that he met the Fourteenth Amendment standard because tribal members were subject to some part of the laws of the United States and thus he was born "subject to the jurisdiction" of the United States. But as shown in the preceding chapter that claim that a "partial jurisdiction" makes one "subject to the jurisdiction" and an entitlement to birthright citizenship had been anticipated and rejected in debates on the Fourteenth Amendment. And now this claim was rejected by the Supreme Court, which distinguished between partial jurisdiction and the full and complete jurisdiction that attaches to birthright citizenship. The "evident meaning" of "subject to the jurisdiction," the Court found, was "not merely subject in some respect or degree to the jurisdiction of the United States, but completely subject to their political jurisdiction, and owing them direct and immediate allegiance."

The postscript to *Elk v. Wilkins* is that its denial of birthright citizenship through the Fourteenth Amendment to Native Americans under tribal government did not for them close the door to citizenship. Congress, by virtue of its several powers — respecting treaties, naturalization, and Native Americans — might otherwise provide them with birthright citizenship. Congress had on occasion done so, by means of treaties with various tribes. Then in 1924 by the Indian Citizenship Act, Congress provided birthright citizenship to all Native Americans irrespective of tribal status.[83]

---

83. Elk v. Wilkins, 112 U.S. 94 (1884); the Indian Citizenship Act is codified at 8 U.S.C. § 1401. At about the same time as *Elk v. Wilkins'* take on partial jurisdiction, the Attorney General issued an opinion to the same effect as that stated in that case, that

# Immigrants

In two different cases, *Benny v. O'Brien* and *United States v. Wong Kim Ark*, the Supreme Court of New Jersey and the United States Supreme Court considered whether immigrants not yet citizens might gain birthright citizenship for their children. In both cases, the courts found that immigrants might well be entitled, indeed were in the circumstances of those cases, to that citizenship. In doing so, both courts clarified our notion of aliens and solidified our notion of immigrants. Also, these two cases, as it turns out, have been the last decisions by the courts on birthright citizenship.

*Benny v. O'Brien*, rendered in 1895 by the Supreme Court of New Jersey, is a well-reasoned decision on birthright citizenship.[84] The question, whether Allan Benny had been born a citizen, arose in an attempt to disqualify him from serving on a municipal board on the grounds he was not a citizen. He had been born in Brooklyn to Scottish parents who had immigrated to the United States and had lived here since, lawfully and permanently. Benny's father had declared his intention to be naturalized, but had not, at the time of the decision, finished the course.

To gain birthright citizenship as provided by the Fourteenth Amendment, "Two facts," the Court stated, "must concur: the person must be born here, and he must be subject to the jurisdiction of the United States." Owing to the subject to jurisdiction requirement, not everyone born in the United States received birthright citizenship. In the words of the Court, the "born in the United States and subject to the jurisdiction thereof" terms of the Amendment "concede that there may be instances in which the right to citizenship does not attach by reason of birth in this country." Among those

---

partial jurisdiction was insufficient for birthright citizenship. This opinion was by Attorney General George Williams, who earlier and as a senator from Oregon had been active in the production of the Fourteenth Amendment. In this opinion, the now Attorney General Williams stated: "Section 1 of the 14th amendment to the Constitution declares that 'all persons born or naturalized in the United States, and subject to the jurisdiction thereof, are citizens of the United States and of the State wherein they reside.' But the word 'jurisdiction' must be understood to mean absolute or complete jurisdiction, such as the United States had over its citizens before the adoption of this amendment. Aliens, among whom are persons born here and naturalized abroad, dwelling or being in this country, are subject to the jurisdiction of the United States only to a limited extent. Political and military rights and duties do not pertain to them." "Expatriation — Foreign Domicile — Citizenship," 14 U.S. Op. Atty. Gen. 295, 300 (1873).

84. Benny v. O'Brien, 58 N.J. Law, at 36 (1895) (New Jersey Supreme Court).

excluded, the Court said, were persons "born in this country of foreign parents who are temporarily traveling here."

The parents of Allan Benny, though, had a connection greater than a "transient presence" with the country. They were clearly here for the long run; here they lived and worked in accordance with the law and were bent on doing so for the rest of their lives. They were, as said by the Court, "domiciled in this country." Accordingly, the Court found that these parents were subject to the jurisdiction of the United States and Alan thus was born as a citizen. The precise holding was that "Allan Benny is a citizen of the United States in virtue of his birth here of alien parents, who at the time of his birth were domiciled in this country." As this holding refers to alien it reifies the concept, relieving it of feudal premises of permanent servitude and placing it within republican premises of immigration, of the opportunity in America to throw off old allegiance, to join the nation, and to be rewarded with birthright citizenship for doing so.

Interestingly, in *Benny v. O'Brien*, the Court in part based its holding, of birthright citizenship for persons domiciled in the United States, on another premise. In the years before the Fourteenth Amendment, the *National Anti-Slavery Standard* stated that African Americans gained US citizenship as they were "persons born on its soil of parents permanently resident there." Were domicile not a basis for citizenship, the Court said in *Benny v. O'Brien*, "the fourteenth amendment has failed to accomplish its purpose, and the colored people are not citizens." The Court further reasoned that inasmuch as domicile was a premise of African American citizenship and inasmuch as that premise — given the egalitarian context of the Fourteenth Amendment — applied to all alike, Scots as well as African Americans, then Benny Allan, also born on US soil to parents permanently resident here, likewise gained birthright citizenship. As said by the Court, "The same rule must be applied to both races."[85]

Before *Benny v. O'Brien*, the fact of being lawfully settled within a nation, which is what domicile is, had already been marked as a way of identifying and affiliating a person with the nation. John Marshall of the US Supreme Court in 1814 spoke of settlement in a nation as establishing a reciprocal set of obligations. Citing Emir de Vattel (as discussed in Chapter 3 earlier), the Chief Justice noted that domicile requires "not only actual residence, but 'an intention of always staying there.'" Marshall then further

---

85. Benny v. O'Brien, 58 N.J. Law at 40. Shortly thereafter in United States v. Wong Kim Ark, 169 U.S. 649 (1898) as I shall discuss, the United States Supreme Court quoted *Benny v. O'Brien* on this point, that as domicile was the basis of extending citizenship to African American, then so that basis, domicile, extended to everyone.

noted that domicile thus defined gives rise to reciprocal obligations, on the part of the individual to the nation and vice versa. In return for its long-term protection of permanent residents, the nation might reasonably well demand greater contributions, including the "oblig[ation] to defend" the nation, from them. As they meet these contributive responsibilities, permanent legal residents might reasonably and reciprocally gain rights on the order of citizens. Under *Benny v. O'Brien* one of these rights is birthright citizenship.

Three years later in 1898 in *United States v. Wong Kim Ark*, by means of a carefully and precisely worded holding, the United States Supreme Court agreed with *Benny v. O'Brien*. The holding was that "a child born in the United States, of parents . . . who . . . have a permanent domicile and residence in the United States, and are there carrying on business . . . becomes at the time of his birth a citizen of the United States." That holding stands as the last ruling by any United States Court on birthright citizenship under the Fourteenth Amendment. And now we cover that holding in detail.

The claimant who gained citizenship, one Wong Kim Ark, was a Chinese laborer born and residing in San Francisco. When he visited China and tried to return to the United States, his reentry was barred by immigration officials because he was precluded from doing so by the "Chinese Exclusion Act." That Act precluded entry by Chinese laborers: Not all Chinese, not merchants or professionals but laborers, which Kim was and accordingly his reentry was for the moment barred. The professed but not necessarily the entire reason for the Act's preclusion of Chinese laborers was to limit the "coolie" system of indentured immigration (if not servitude) then practiced in China. For a fee, indigents in China were collected by Chinese organizations, the "Seven Corporations" as they were known, and then shipped abroad to the United States, Australia, South America, and the Caribbean. The indigent was expected to pay this fee out of his earnings. If not paid, his family in China was held as security for the fee and stood to be sold to secure payment. All of which was a system that we might well choose to avoid. Be that as it may, Chinese labor was also opposed on other grounds, as by American labor unions and as by cultural and ethnic objections. As summarized by the Supreme Court, the latter objection was to the "large numbers of Chinese laborers, of a distinct race and religion, remaining strangers in the land, residing apart by themselves, tenaciously adhering to the customs and usages of their own country, unfamiliar with our institutions, and apparently incapable of assimilating with our people."[86] These concerns about assimilation, we now know, were unfounded. Given their

---

86. Fong Yue Ting v. United States, 149 U.S. 698, 717 (1893). For an account of the Coolie system, *see* Cong. Globe, 41st Cong. 2d Sess. 4275–77 (1874). Labor unions

contributions to our society and qualities such as a good regard for family, community, and education, the Chinese were not and are not at all strangers.

Whatever the reason for the exclusion of Chinese laborers, that exclusion could not be applied to Wong Kim Ark if he were a citizen and he claimed he was. He said he had been born a citizen. And the Court so held. His parents had come here from China. Although they were not citizens, they were yet lawfully settled in California as immigrants. When Kim was born, they lived and worked in San Francisco as permanent and lawful residents. They were, in the refrain that ran throughout the opinion, of "a permanent domicile and residence in the United States, and are there carrying on business." In terms of *Benny v. O'Brien,* "permanent domicile and residence in the United States" was sufficient for birthright citizenship. But for Wong Kim Ark, there was another fact in play, which might seem to be greatly significant but in fact was not, except for the two dissenting members of the Court.

The fact was: While his parents had a substantial and permanent relation with the United States, they, the parents, could not become citizens. A short way of explaining why is to say that under our Burlingame Treaty with China, the Chinese might immigrate, settle, and do business in the United States as had Wong Kim's parents but could not be naturalized as citizens. The Burlingame Treaty had provided that "nothing herein contained shall be held to confer naturalization on the citizens of the United States in China, nor upon the subjects of China in the United States." Exactly why that provision was included in the treaty is unclear. It may have been insisted on by China. That nation did not tolerate expatriation by its subjects; in China expatriation was punishable by death. Nor was China open to foreigners; accordingly the treaty did not "confer naturalization on the citizens of the United States in China."[87] Otherwise, it was not altogether clear that the treaty permanently barred the Chinese who came here under it from being naturalized as citizens. Sen. Charles Summers had maintained that the "nothing herein contained shall be held to confer naturalization" terms of the treaty meant only that the treaty itself was not an

opposed, but capitalists tended to favor, the immigration. *See* Fred W. Riggs, *Pressures on Congress: A Study of the Repeal of Chinese Exclusion* (1950).

87. Burlingame Treaty, July 28, 1868, 16 Stat. 740. Stated more fully, the treaty provided that "Citizens of the United States visiting or residing in China,... and, reciprocally, Chinese subjects visiting or residing in the United States, shall enjoy the same privileges, immunities, and exemptions, in respect to travel or residence, as may there be enjoyed by the citizens or subjects of the most favored nation. But nothing herein contained shall be held to confer naturalization upon citizens of the United States in China, nor upon the subjects of China in the United States."

act of naturalization and that at best those terms were a rather a holding action, "until such time as the Chinese who came here adapted to republican government."

Be that as it may, over time attitudes hardened — so that by the time of *United States v. Wong Kim Ark* Chinese were barred from being naturalized as citizens. Starting with the Immigration and Naturalization Act of 1790, naturalization was open, but only to "any alien, being a free white person." The "free white person" qualification was meant to exclude persons of African descent. However, shortly after the Fourteenth Amendment was enacted, Congress by a new and separate enactment opened naturalization to persons of African descent. The 1868 enactment provided that "the naturalization laws are hereby extended to aliens of African nativity, and to persons of African descent." At the same time, though, the "free white persons" terms of the 1790 Act remained in the law on the books. But while those terms remained on the book, their "preclusion of African Americans" purpose had been eliminated. Accordingly, the free white person part of the 1790 Act might well be treated as having been effectively extinguished and that claim was made in cases, *In re Ah Yup* in particular, that involved the Chinese. Be that as it may, in *In re Ah Yup* and notwithstanding that the original purpose for the "free white persons" proviso had been eliminated, the court held that as those provisions remained on the books the proviso applied to and precluded naturalization of the Chinese. (This take on "white persons" had a checkered application; it restricted Asians but apparently no others. For instance, in *In re Rodriguez* the contention was that under the white persons provision of the 1790 Act, a Mexican citizen, "because of his color," was ineligible for naturalization. That contention was rejected. In the words of the court, "congress retained the word 'white' in the naturalization laws for the sole purpose of excluding the Chinese from the right of naturalization." Accordingly, Rodriquez, being Hispanic rather than Chinese, was counted as a white person and was not excluded.[88] Our exclusion of Asians continued until World War II, a story beyond the scope of this book.)

Although the Burlingame Treaty did not allow for the naturalization of the Chinese, it was a basis for certain entitlements. The treaty denoted "the mutual advantage of the free migration and emigration" of peoples of China

---

88. In re Rodriguez, 81 F. 337 (D.C. Tex. 1897). The Chinese were excluded because they were not white person in In re Ah Yup, 1 F. Cas. 223 (C.C.D. Cal. 1878). The Chinese Exclusion Act may be found at Act of July 14, 1870, ch. 255, 16 Stat. 256 § 7. Regarding the end, during World War II, of the exclusion from naturalization of Asians, *see* the Act of Dec. 17, 1943, ch. 344, 57 Stat. 600.

and the United States and then provided that "Chinese subjects visiting or residing in the United States, shall enjoy the same privileges, immunities, and exemptions in respect to travel or residence, as may there be enjoyed by the citizens or subjects of the most favored nation." These treaty-based privileges were turned into guarantees of equal civil rights — particularly for the Chinese — by the Civil Rights Act of 1870.[89] But while the Chinese might settle here and were guaranteed civil rights, they could not be naturalized as citizens. Amidst this welter, Wong Kim Ark brought his case.

Born here to Chinese immigrants, he claimed citizenship not by a route of naturalization but as a birthright provided by the Fourteenth Amendment. Although his parents had not lived here as citizens, they had lived here in the manner of citizens. Accordingly, for Wong Kim Ark and his parents, the holding was that "a child born in the United States, of parents . . . who . . . have a permanent domicile and residence in the United States, and are there carrying on business . . . becomes at the time of his birth a citizen of the United States." Wong Kim Ark's parents were substantially connected to the United States and the Court's holding recited that connection.[90] The holding, as presented in the last part of the opinion, was that the Court had been presented a "single question." The "intention, and the necessary effect, of the submission of this case to the decision of the

---

89. In In re Ah Chong, 2 F. 733 (D. Ca. 1880), the court barred California from denying fishing rights to Chinese immigrants, on the grounds that that denial violated the Burlingame Treaty and equal protection of law as provided by the Fourteenth Amendment. Regarding the Civil Rights Act of 1870, ch. 114, §§ 16 & 17, 16 Stat. 140, *see* Charles J. McClain, Jr., The Chinese Struggle for Civil Rights in Nineteenth Century America: The First Phase, 1850–1870, 72 *Cal. L. Rev.* 529, 566 (1984). In Runyon v. McClary, 427 U.S. 168, 200 (1976), Justice White explained the Act's purpose, quoting from congressional debate on it as follows: "[W]e will protect Chinese aliens or any other aliens whom we allow to come here, and give them a hearing in our courts; let them sue and be sued; let them be protected by all the laws."

90. However, the majority opinion, written by Justice Grey, included a lengthy discourse considerably wide of that holding that today is wrongly cited for a reductive view of the Fourteenth Amendment, the view being that the Amendment adopted *Calvin's Case* as the measure of birthright citizenship in America. Here Grey's remarks, as opposed to the Court's holding, may have been prompted by a certain hard-edged argument that had apparently been advanced by a San Francisco attorney, George Collins, who had joined the case and argued against Wong Kim Ark's citizenship. As said by Justice Grey, "one of the learned counsel for the United States" contended that an *exclusive* rule of descent from citizen parents was required by the Fourteenth Amendment. Grey dismissed that contention but did so by bad historical reasoning that is not worth repeating. The reason I do not is that the holding in *Wong Kim Ark* does not include Grey's bad use of history.

court upon the facts agreed by the parties, were to present for determination the single question. . . ." The single question was "namely, whether a child born in the United States, of parents of Chinese descent, who, at the time of his birth, are subjects of the emperor of China, but have a permanent domicile and residence in the United States, and are there carrying on business . . . becomes at the time of his birth a citizen of the United States." The holding that then followed was:

> The amendment, in clear words and in manifest intent, includes the children born within the territory of the United States of all other persons, of whatever race or color, domiciled within the United States. Every citizen or subject of another country, while domiciled here, is within the allegiance and the protection, and consequently subject to the jurisdiction, of the United States.

About this holding, please note: First, it is about the Fourteenth Amendment, about its "words" and "intent." Second, it is about and turns on the Amendment's "subject to the jurisdiction" standard. Third, by this holding "allegiance" is an essential part of "subject to the jurisdiction." Fourth, allegiance is inferred from "domicile," being lawfully settled in the United States.

*United States v. Wong Kim Ark's* holding about birthright citizenship is limited to those whom we now refer to as "LPRs." As earlier noted, LPRs are legal permanent residents, as immigrants lawfully and permanently residing in the United States and are deserving particular consideration because they are, as the modern Court has said, "in so many respects situated similarly to citizens."[91]

The dissent in *United States v. Wong Kim Ark* agreed that a child born to parents permanently and lawfully residing in the United States received citizenship. It agreed that "the proper construction" of the Fourteenth Amendment was "that all persons born in the United States of parents permanently residing here, and susceptible of becoming citizens, are citizens." It differed from the majority because the dissent objected to the "susceptible of becoming citizens" part of the majorities holding. While Wong Kim Ark's parents were lawfully and permanently settled here, yet by our treaty with China we had pledged they would not be made citizens. Accordingly, the United States could not, as the dissent put it, in this special case of a

---

91. Toll v. Moreno, 458 U.S. 1, 44 (1982). And as also previously noted, LPRs are defined, at 8 U.S.C.A. § 1101(a)(20) as "the status of having been lawfully accorded the privilege of residing permanently in the United States as an immigrant in accordance with the immigration laws, such status not having changed."

treaty provision go about "imposing" citizenship on their children. The point is not that the dissent correctly or incorrectly construed the effect of the Burlington Treaty on birthright citizenship. Instead, the point is that otherwise the dissent was in agreement with the majority's holding that a "citizen or subject of another country, while domiciled here, is within the allegiance and the protection, and consequently subject to the jurisdiction, of the United States." On this point, the opinion in *United States v. Wong Kim Ark* is unanimous and in accord with *Benny v. O'Brien*.

# Chapter Seven

# Birthright Citizenship and the Civic Minimum

A republic entails "a strong sense of morality,
of fairness, or aversion to unfairness."

Vetterli and Bryner, *In Search of the Republic* (1996)
(quoting Robert A. Goodwin)

"Citizenship in this Nation is a part of a cooperative affair. Its
citizenry is the country and the country is its citizenry."

Afroyim v. Rusk, 387 U.S. 253 (1967)

Throughout this book I refer to a virtue that binds to a citizenry. About it, this virtue, a phrase that comes to mind is "cardinal value." "Cardinal" is best understood by reference to its Latin root, which is *cardo* (meaning hinge). Therefore, the *cardinal* virtues in their various expressions—benevolence, patience, fortitude, industry, and the like—are those on which our civic order turns. Throughout the book, these virtues are presented and praised. But to know where exactly virtue comes from, this chapter might help.

An assertion at the time of our Revolution, by Samuel Adams, was that "our enemies have made it an Object, to eradicate from the Minds of the People in general a Sense of true religion and Virtue, in hopes thereby the more easily to carry their point of enslaving them." His cousin John Adams more peacefully made the same point, saying "Liberty can no more exist without virtue . . . than the body can exist without a soul." These indispensable virtues were then variously stated in basic public documents, as by the Virginia Declaration of Rights of 1776 that proclaimed "No free government . . . can be preserved to any people, but by a firm adherence to justice, moderation, temperance, and virtue" or by the Massachusetts Bill of Rights that affirmed that "a constant adherence to . . . piety, justice, moderation, temperance, industry, and frugality, are absolutely necessary to preserve the advantages of liberty, and to maintain free government." Generally speaking, we followed Montesquieu on the point that "virtue is the principle of a republican government" and (backhandedly) Hobbes on the point that without virtue despotic government is in order. That these cardinal virtues are essential to democratic society is substantiated by a finely reasoned body of philosophical and historical work. And truth is told by religious conviction: As said by Montesquieu, "If faith be wanting he must be a subject; and if he be free he must believe."[92]

All of which is true, but virtue as we know it also has a scientific basis. The philosophy, friendship, and faith that account for virtue are, as we should know, abetted and proved by social and biological data. Humankind is complex, mixing the capacity to live well with the chance to live badly. Essential traits, of say altruism, are not uniformly distributed. (The idea of fallen comes to mind.) Hence, the capacity to live well needs to be cultivated lest it die among the weeds of people living badly. About that care, of human nature, the science of human nature, provides some pointers.

Studies show that by evolutionary processes, we have been fitted with moral traits that are essential to an optimal existence on this planet. These traits, as we shall see, are often expressed in terms of altruism and strong altruism and reciprocity and strong reciprocity. As thus expressed, they include the cardinal virtues. Strong reciprocity, though, has a hard edge, of not suffering wrongdoing, not ordinarily be associated with virtue, but it, as we will see, is. Altogether, these traits, of altruism and reciprocity, go toward assuring what Stuart White identifies as the "civic minima" for the

---

92. Charles (Baron) De Montesquieu, *The Spirit of the Laws* (1748) discussing the separation of powers, generally citing the Roman Republic as an example. The Adams' statements about virtue are found at Richard Vetterle & Gary Bryner, *In Search of the Republic: Public Virtue and the Root of American Government,* 77 (1996). The quote by Tocqueville is at 110 of that book. About faith and democracy, Tocqueville further said that American's "combine the notions of Christianity and of liberty so intimately in their minds that it is impossible to make them conceive the one without the other. . . . I have known them of societies formed by American to send out ministers of the Gospel into the new Western states, to found schools and churches there, lest religion should be allowed to die away in those remote settlements, and the rising states be less fitted to enjoy free institutions than the people from whom they came." *id.* at 114. (p. 436 *Democracy in America,* 1831). *See* Robert Bellah, Civil Religion in America, 96 *J. Am. Acad. Arts Sci.* 1–21 (1967).

modern democratic state.[93] As such, they are essential to sustaining our citizenry and help us understand how birthright citizenship may add to or detract from that sustenance.

# Fairness as Reciprocity

Going through relevant studies about immigrants and birthright citizenship, it can be seen that birthright citizenship is not exclusively reserved for US citizens. Immigrants lawfully settled within the United States are also entitled to it. In their gut, few citizens disagree with that entitlement. (One reason I can say so is that reform bills presently offered in Congress commonly provide citizenship to these immigrants.) The question is why and how our civic conscience works in such a way that few of us disagree with an entitlement to citizenship to these immigrants? The answer no doubt sounds in a sense that these immigrants *fairly* gain citizenship. They pay taxes, are subject to military service, and are under a duty of loyalty (they are subject to our law respecting treason), all the same as the rest of us.[94] In return, they are fairly entitled to citizenship.

"In return" and "fairly" are easily and naturally linked, in the preceding sentence, because for human being reciprocity is fairness. It is a truth clear enough to be embedded in language, as in "turn-about is fair play" or "one good turn deserves another," or, simply, "in return." Without and not needing formal proof, Cicero asserted, "There is no duty more indispensable than that of returning a kindness." (And as he added, "all men distrust one forgetful of a benefit.") While the relation of fairness to reciprocity is clear enough not to need philosophical proof, still modern political philosophy adds to what we might not intuit, which is how that relation is essential to modern democracy. For instance, in *A Theory of Justice* (1971), John Rawls famously spoke of "fairness as reciprocity," and affirmed that a "conception of justice is stable" when "citizens" see "that others are committed to our good, that as we make contributions to them we can expect as much from them." In his book on moral philosophy (entitled *Reciprocity* (1986)), Lawrence Becker posited that "equilibrium" in a good society requires that it "cultivate the disposition to reciprocate, fittingly and proportionately." Just

---

93. Stuart White, *The Civic Minimum: On the Rights and Obligations of Economic Citizenship* (2003).

94. *See* 26 U.S.C. §7701 (2007) (taxation on domestic and worldwide income); 50 U.S.C. § 453(a) (military service); Carlisle v. United States, 83 U.S. 147, 155 (1873) (duty of loyalty).

how this works, that fairness as reciprocity is essential to stable civic societies (at least when they are free) is shown by reference to facts of human nature. Among others, Stuart White has noted this linkage, saying that the civic minimum for a democracy depends on a "democratic mutual regard," a respect of citizen for citizens that is "intrinsic and rooted in their common humanity."

According to Hobbes, that sort of mutual regard is far too scarce in human beings; we are too egoistic therefore the Leviathan. On this side of the Atlantic, though, our assumptions are different and were so from the beginning. The settlers at Plymouth had sailed outside the reach of that beast. At Plymouth, they were for practical purposes beyond the power of James I, that power being limited by "the remote distances of those places." But those settlers were not therefore at a loss. Immediately, they provided for self-government. By the Mayflower Compact, they did "covenant and combine ourselves together into a Civil Body Politick," the end of which was "the General good." Covenants of that kind are one thing, carrying them out another. By Hobbesian accounts of human nature, we are too selfish to do so. Hobbes, though, had after all not fully accounted for human nature. A fuller accounting has been a modern project, entailing studies out of various disciplines, such as anthropology, evolutionary psychology, and public choice and attendant game theory. The amount and consistency of these studies are such the initial skepticism of them, expressed as "scratch an altruist and watch a hypocrite bleed," has been dispelled.

Some of these studies show the accomplished fact of innate and mutually supporting traits of altruism and reciprocity; others are about the accomplishment itself, through evolution, of these traits. To these various studies, the problem known as the prisoner's dilemma is a good point of entry. The problem came out of work in the 1950s by the Rand Corporation, a group that tried to understand and deal with the problem of proliferation of nuclear weapons among nations. In time, the dilemma was cast in the form of a prisoner's dilemma and as such proliferated — it is the subject of perhaps two thousand scholarly works — in that it smartly sets up the problem of coordination among rationally self-interested persons. The problem, familiar if for no other reason than the long-running television series, Law and Order, is as follows: Two suspected accomplices in a crime are detained by the police, kept in separate rooms, and not allowed to talk to each other. Each is then offered this deal. If one testifies against the other and the other remains silent, one (the betrayer) goes free and the other (stand-up guy) gets a ten-year sentence. If both testify against each other, they both receive five-year sentences. However, if both remain silent, both are sentenced to only six months on a minor charge.

So how should they, as rationally self-interested persons, respond? The answer, as it turns out, is not with the best but with the suboptimal, second-best response. The best response is to remain silent and gain the six-month sentence. But by consensus that is not the "rational" response. The rational response is the inferior one of betrayal. By this choice, no matter what the other prisoner does the one is better-off by cutting a ten-year sentence down to five year. Consequently, mutual betrayal is the logical outcome.[95] The implications of this rational solution are considerable and considerably occur. Athletes and steroids are an example. Given the health risk, the optimal action is not to take these drugs. But as there are cheaters seeking a competitive advantage, the calculation changes so that in order to keep up, all take steroids, all then gain no competitive advantage and all suffer health injury. In this way, rational choice has produced a suboptimal solution in some sports, for instance baseball in what is now known as its steroid era.

What I presented so far, though, is the prisoner's dilemma in simple form. A more complicated and true-to-life form replicates social living within communities and here the solution changes. In this form the dilemma is iterated. It is not an isolated incident but occurs time and again. And it reoccurs among players who remember one another and choices made in previous encounters. In this form of relations over time, the dilemma better approximates community life. Respecting this form, Robert Axelrod arranged for a computer-played tournament, where the dilemma was iterated, among a large number of players. The purpose of this contest was to learn the strategy most favorable to the individual player. Each submitted a strategy; and the strategies thus collected were then played against each other through computer programs. Out of this contest came a really good book, *The Evolution of Cooperation* (1984). In that book, Axelrod first asks whether the cooperation that is essential to social living might not have come about through natural selection. At the end, the conclusion was yes, stated in terms of "no central authority is needed: cooperation based on reciprocity can be self-policing."

In the tournament itself—in the iterating context that better replicates social living—the winning strategy was the simplest strategy, which was "tit for tat." By this strategy, a player's first response in the first game is to cooperate rather than to betray. In subsequent games, however, players

---

95. Unless it is the case that the partners selected each other based on each being steadfast, of being "cooperators" (true one to another) rather than a defectors (betrayers) and in which case they remain silent. This is referred to as the "super rational solution," which, in life, may be a citizenry. We will discuss more about it later.

respond according to what one's partner did in previous games. If the other player had betrayed him before, that player in turn now stands to be treated likewise. Out of tit for tat, there are lessons for social living. If you know nothing of a person, first do well by him or her. Thereafter, though, do not be a sap (sap here being susceptible of a technical definition). If you fail to retaliate for known bad behavior, bad actors, and in this life there are enough of them, will keep at you. In time they stand to damage not just you but the whole community. In part they may do so by steadily appropriating and depleting the stock of public goods, such as social insurance, created by the community for the good of the whole. But worse than material goods, they stand to destroy the disposition essential to creating those goods; we will know more about it later.

## Strong Altruism

Altruism refers to a capacity to act with and for the benefit of others. In its "weak" form (which is enlightened self-interest), a person acts with no particular expectation of a return but with the knowledge that a return of some sort, for instance a good reputation, is likely. In academia, scholars may on this basis read and provide hopefully helpful comments on each other's work. In this weak form, we speak of humankind as "*homo economicus*," the self-interested but yet enlightened person who understands that good deeds produce personal gain and acts accordingly. As previously noted at the beginning of this chapter, in his work *Democracy in America*, Alexis de Tocqueville wrote, "The Americans . . . are fond of explaining almost all the actions of their lives by the principle of self-interest rightly understood; they show with complacency how an enlightened regard for themselves constantly prompts them to assist one another and inclines them willingly to sacrifice a portion of their time and property to the welfare for the state."

But by no means does this weak form, *homo economicus*, account for the full range of altruism. The full range includes "strong altruism." Here people generously give their time and money and perhaps their life and do so without the thought or chance of repayment. Tocqueville did not miss this stronger form. When he referred to enlightened self-interest, he understood this was an incomplete picture of American society. Accordingly, he added that "in the United States as well as elsewhere people sometimes seem to give way to those disinterested and spontaneous impulses that are natural to man." Thus, Tocqueville identified strong altruism, as in fact did the great doubter, Hobbes himself, who had noted as an odd sort of fact that his gift of six-pence to a needful old man "doth also relieve me." Today, the emotion Hobbes noted is identified not as a stray impulse but as an innate and evolved part of human nature. This fuller specification of the provenance — the genetic and evolution basis — of strong altruism comes to us largely from evolutionary psychology.

The seminal insight that identified strong altruism and anchored it in natural selection was that of Robert L. Trivers, himself trained as a biologist. Trivers both showed and explained reciprocal altruism by references to birds and the fact that they whistle warnings of a predator despite risking their life in doing so. They did so because those calls were in their genes. Trivers's succinct explanation of the evolutionary basis of that behavior was as follows: "It does not matter that in giving a warning call the caller is helping its neighbors more than it is helping itself. What counts is that it outcompetes conspecifics from areas in which no one is giving warning calls. The non-calling neighbors of the caller . . . will soon find themselves in an area without any caller and will be selected against relative to birds in an area with callers." Natural selection, therefore, "favor[ed] the spread of the warning call genes." As then shown by Trivers, and by any number of subsequent studies, the selflessness that produced those warning calls is also at home among the human species, as an adaptive trait that contributes to the well-being of the species.[96]

But before Trivers proved it, we actually knew it. In 1810, Chief Justice Parsons of the Massachusetts Supreme Court was called on to address, in a case before him, the civic possibilities, or not, of religious morality.[97] In this respect and for his conspecifics, Parsons found that "charity and

---

96. Robert L. Trivers, The Evolution of Reciprocal Altruism, 46 Q. Rev. Biol. 35 (1971). Subsequent studies about reciprocal altruism and the evolution basis of it are numerous. Of these studies, some are particularly relevant to citizenship in that they focus more on how reciprocal altruism contributes to civic associations. Of these studies, the work of Samuel Bowles & Herbert Gintis is especially pertinent as it relates altruism and its associated trait of reciprocity to civic living. See Samuel Bowles & Herbert Gintis, Behavioural Sciences: Homo Reciprocan, Nature, Jan. 2002 at 125–28 and Samuel Bowles & Herbert Gintis, Is Equality Passé? Boston Review, Dec. 1998/Jan. 1999. Also particularly relevant is Jerome H. Barkow, et al., The Adapted Mind: Evolutionary Psychology and the Generation of Culture, 207 (1991).

97. Justice Parsons's dissertation was in Barnes v. Inhabitants of First Parish in Falmouth, 6 Mass. 401, 405–06 (1810). More fully, Parsons wrote:

Human laws cannot oblige to the performance of the duties of imperfect obligation; as the duties of charity and hospitality, benevolence and good neighborhood; as the duties resulting from the relation of husband and wife, parent and child; of man to man, as children of a common parent; and of real patriotism, by influencing every citizen to love his country, and to obey all its laws. These are moral duties, flowing from the disposition of the heart, and not subject to the control of human legislation.

hospitality, benevolence and good neighborhood" and "real patriotism," were obligations not necessarily or at times even possibly commanded by law. Instead and more reliably these qualities "flow[ed] from the disposition of the heart." In these terms, strong altruism is essential to good political communities. For them the protection of law is necessary but not sufficient. Enforcers of the law cannot be everywhere and the law itself, given our imperfect prescience and the limitations of language, does not in all situations ordain the right outcome. Also, from primitive villages to the modern democratic state, political communities have provided public goods, as in communal food storage provided by Native American tribes in the Pacific Northwest or public education as provided by all of our present fifty states. These goods depend on contribution by the community.[98]

The point increasingly made by social scientists is that, as Justice Parsons understood, society requires an extra-legal commitment of the moral mind. The point hard to overstate is that this commitment is open ended. It does not consist, as might a deontologically determined order, of a specified set of obligations and rights. Rather, the commitment is that of an unrestricted benevolence — from the heart — that better meets the contingencies and varying prospects of the human condition. As put by Lawrence Becker in *Reciprocity*, as "rational agents" we must "return good for the good we get"; we must do so in order to "sustain the sort of equilibrium necessary for productive social intercourse." Therefore, "social structures should be designed to be consistent with the obligations of reciprocity and, relatedly, so as to cultivate the disposition to reciprocate, fittingly and proportionately" and to do so by means of "exchange over time." In that sentence, fittingly, proportionately, and exchange over time are luminous concepts and capacities.

---

Neither can the laws prevent, by temporal punishment, secret offences, committed without witness, to gratify malice, revenge, or any other passion, by assailing the most important and most estimable rights of others. For human tribunals cannot proceed against any crimes, unless ascertained by evidence; and they are destitute of all power to prevent the commission of offences, unless by the feeble examples exhibited in the punishment of those who may be detected.

Government, therefore, availing itself only of its own powers, is extremely defective; and unless it could derive assistance from some superior power, whose laws extend to the temper and disposition of the human heart, and before whom no offence is secret, wretched indeed would be the state of man under a civil constitution of any form.

98. Regarding provision of public goods in more primitive societies, *see* Allen W. Johnson & Timothy Earle, *The Evolution of Human Societies: From Foraging Group to Agrarian State* (2d ed. 2000).

# Strong Reciprocity

As said by Marc Hauser in his book *Moral Minds*, the "lesson for human beings is that our frequent use of reciprocity in society may be an inevitable part of our natures: an instinct. We do not need to reason to the conclusion that 'one good turn deserves another'. . . . It simply develops within us as we mature, in ineradicable predisposition, to be nurtured by teaching or not as the case may be. And why? Because natural selection has chosen it to enable us to get more from social living." Today no one doubts this instinct. This instinct does, though, take us in perhaps an unexpected direction.

The case remains that humans are not angels, which is to say that traits of selfless cooperation are not uniformly distributed. Cheaters do abound and, by taking unfair advantage, they stand to increase within a community to cause deterioration by exploiting more selfless persons. After they run down the community, these cheaters might themselves form a new community. But that community will be unstable. Once they have used up the resources produced by their hosts, cheaters stand to turn on each other so all that is possible is a Hobbesian community where life is only somewhat better than nasty, brutish, and short.

It is the case, then, that altruistic traits should be conserved, certainly where the democratic state is the goal. It is here, in keeping with this conservation, that strong altruism takes what is perhaps a surprising turn. It includes not just acting with and for others; it also includes — and identifies as prologue to virtue — acting against, as by punishing, those who violate social norms and do so even though that punishment is costly to the punisher. This is referred to as strong reciprocity. As technically defined, "Strong reciprocity arises when members of a social group . . . are willing to punish violators even when the act of punishment is costly and there is no opportunity to see the person again."[99]

As it is noted that punishment is costly to the donor as well as the recipient, this definition includes an aspect of punishment we do not often consider: Why do we, anyway, punish others for their wrongs to strangers when that punishment is costly to us? Why may it be felt as just? The answer is that accepting bad deeds runs altruism down. As the punishment feature of reciprocal altruism is suppressed, the disposition itself, the willingness to give of oneself for the benefit of others, is stunted. In civic terms, a "sense of fairness — and a willingness to punish the unfair even at

---

99. Marc D. Hauser, *The Moral Mind* (2006). And *see* Ernst Fehr & Simon Gächter, Altruistic Punishment in Humans, *Nature,* Jan. 2002, at 415, 137–40.

some cost to oneself . . . is what allows large social groups to form." And as is added, "free-riders would ruin such groups, because playing fair would cease to have any value."[100]

Anthropology shows this, as do laboratory conditions that consist of public goods games. In these games people play for gain and do so in varying circumstances, both with neighbors (those with whom they work in repeated games) and with strangers. In these games, a player may take all or some part of an available good. Taking all the good, however, denies the other players any share of it. In those circumstances, the players as a rule take only a fair share; they leave something for other players. But in these public goods games as in life, not all players are altruistic. Some (usually about 25%) take unfair shares as best they can. When the rules are such that the altruistic players must abide these abusers — when they cannot expel or otherwise take action against them — over time the (formerly) altruistic players commence to play selfishly. And generosity withers.

An observation much to the same effect is about, what else, recycling. Self-estimates of recycling are often inaccurate. However, people do accurately assess their neighbors' recycling. In turn, estimates of the neighbors' efforts turn out to be reasonably accurate indicators of one's own recycling. Thus, this inference: "People are recycling a certain percentage because that is the percentage they perceive their neighbor is recycling. The degree to which people in a community are willing to engage in cooperative behavior . . . is dependent upon whether or not one perceives others in the community as playing by the same rules."[101] For baseball, it was with regard to the righteousness of the game that by a barely perceptible tip of his cap Roger Clemens accepted as due, for his own beaning of Mets catcher Mike Piazza, the pitch (somewhat) thrown at him at Shea Stadium on June 15, 2007.

Punishment simply entails imposing costs on offenders; these costs vary, as from gossip to scolding to expulsion from a group, much as bicyclers exclude shirkers from the peloton. Within the peloton, lead bikers take on the full force of head winds, shielding those behind, and in doing so they work harder. These riders withstand the wind for a while and then move back into the pack and others take their place. The net result is a collective gain in speed for the peloton. But then there are free riders, who try to save

---

100. Samuel Bowles & Herbert Gintis, Behavioural Sciences: Homo Reciprocan, *Nature*, Jan. 2002, at 415, 125–28; Patience, Fairness, and the Human Condition, The Economist, Oct. 2007. *See also* Ernst Fehr & Simon Gächter, Altruistic Punishment in Humans, *Nature*, Jan. 2002, at 415, 137–40.

101. E. Donald Elliott, Law and Biology: The New Synthesis, 41 *St. Louis U. L.J.* 595, 611 (1997).

their energy by not taking the lead. When found out, these riders are expelled from the peloton and become worse off. Lesser and flexible costs, such as gossip, are enabled by correlative human traits, such as guilt, shame, and embarrassment. In the least, offenders should be refused a free pass, which refusal is an authentically human response. But while a free pass is not in order, forgiveness is. Recall the solution to the prisoner's dilemma, by which bad acts are relentlessly punished but with the actor forgiven (he receives the same deal as the trustworthy) once he begins to act fairly.

What kinds of conclusions may be drawn from this about strong reciprocity as it reinforces altruism by including a disposition to punishment of cheaters? Here is one, again from Stuart White's account in *The Civic Minimum* of the condition essentials to the liberal democratic state. In his words, "resistance to the American welfare state derives not from an opposition to egalitarian redistribution per se, but to redistribution that enables citizens to evade the contributive responsibilities that derive from a widely shared norm." Here is another, by Bowles and Gintis: "Individuals tend not to conform to the standard model of 'Homo economicus,' who rationally pursue his self-interest without regard to any norms of fairness. The evidence rather supports an alternative mode of 'Homo reciprocals.' People tend not to be rational egotists, or unconditional altruists, but conditional cooperators, willing to do their bit in cooperative ventures to which they belong, provided they are assured that others will also make a reasonable contribution. Their commitment to such norms of fairness is such that they are often willing to accept to costs to themselves rather than see such norms violated."

The cohesion of a democratic society turns on a good measure of altruism and regard of one member for another. To altruism and that regard, fairness, that is fairness as reciprocity is important. It is not just important it is authentic. This is why and how John Rawls presented "fairness as reciprocity" and affirmed that a "conception of justice is stable" when "citizens" see "that others are committed to our good, that as we make contributions to them we can expect as much from them." And why and how Stuart White posited that the civic minimum for a democracy depends on a "democratic mutual regard." For this book, the question is how this innate sense of fairness cashes in as it comes to birthright citizenship. This question is continued in the next chapter.

Before the next chapter, though, one more thing: The possibility of living well, that is, within a citizenry, is one of evolution's gifts. This chapter has been about how that possibility is realized. As we may fail, as that possibility is not realized, what then? One "what then" is that we revert to autocratic government. A technical definition of this devolution, out of modern social studies as I have been reviewing, is that "If one removed from evolutionary history and hence from our minds the possibility and cooperation and reciprocity—of mutually contingent benefit-benefit interactions arrived at through mutual consent—then coercion and force would loom even larger as instruments of social influence."[102]

---

102. Cognitive Adaptations for Social Exchange, Leda Cosmides & John Tooby, *The Adapted Mind: Evolutionary Psychology and the Generation of Culture*, 207 (Jerome Barkow et al., eds., 1991).

## Chapter Eight

# Immigration and the Constitutional Standard

Now we move to an urgent point of contact, where the rubber must at last meet the road, where if we have any conviction at all respecting citizenry, the terms of it must now be applied. This point of contact is at and about a social order that has formed in this country, consisting of the millions, a number that however estimated approximates the population of New England, that are within this country in disregard of our laws respecting immigration. As this book goes to press, these numbers, with them we are the world leader, are again of concern.

The United States has a long and poorly secured border with Mexico. Although it is not the only source of illegal immigrations (a number of people are unlawfully here by overstaying their visas), the border is far and away the greater source. Across the border come terrorists and people from around the world, but mainly the crossings are by people from Mexico and Central America.[103] All crossings are often aided by human smuggling enterprises that for a fee assist unlawful immigrants, distribute them across the country, and provide them forged social security cards. These enterprises are comingled with drug smuggling and are on the whole a sordidly criminal business. In 2010, *The New York Times* and *CNN* reported of seventy-two people found murdered in a pipeline, apparently by smugglers, on a ranch in Mexico, and officials assigned to investigate the case were also killed. However, the circumstances of unlawful trafficking while of some pertinence are not particularly the subject matter of this book. The relation of persons who

---

103. In re Rodriguez, 81 F. 33 (D.C. Tex. 1897); Mae M. Ngai, Impossible Subjects, Illegal Aliens and the Making of Modern America 7, 53–54 (2004).

unlawfully entered the country to the citizens of this country is the subject matter, and to that relation we now turn. But first, we present a restatement of some basics.

Sovereignty, the discernment that lest we live as animals we all live under government, is essential. What is not essential is any particular form of it, which in the case of Algernon Sydney was a truth he died for, his offending statement being "God leaves to Man the choice of Forms."[104] For that and similar heresies, Sydney was executed in 1683 at the hands of Charles II, who had continued the claim of his grandfather James I that the form of sovereignty is chosen not by people but is ordained by God and the form so ordained is monarchy. On this side of the Atlantic, we understood that Sydney, and not Charles II, was right and we fought for that cause. But while we understand that humankind is free to choose among forms of sovereignty, we also know that the choice once made includes particular commitments. As the choice is republic as was ours, it requires a gathering of upright people committed to each other. It requires a citizens and that we sustain them. In this respect and as forthrightly shown and stated by Prof. Michael Walzer in *Spheres of Justice: A Defense of Pluralism and Equality* (1983), an obligation of a democratic government is choosing citizens. As Prof. Walzer put it, "Admission and exclusion are at the core of communal independence. They suggest the deepest meaning of self-determination. Without them, there could not be . . . historically stable, ongoing associations of men and women with some special commitment to one another and some special sense of their common life."

Accordingly, the United States like any other nation has standards respecting membership. Ours come from two sources. One is birthright

---

104. At his execution, Sydney was unrepentant, saying: "And I am persuaded to believe that God had left nations to the liberty of setting up such governments as best pleased themselves, and that magistrates were set up for the good of nations, not nations for the honor and glory of magistrates". Algernon Sidney, *Colonel Sidney's Speech Delivered to the sheriff on the scaffold* (December 7, 1683). John and Samuel Adams, George Mason, James Madison, and Benjamin Franklin all acknowledged Sidney's influence on American political thought. A group of Virginians founded Hampden-Sydney College in 1776 and named it in his honor (and John Hampden's). In 1825 and on the occasion of founding the University of Virginia, Thomas Jefferson provided this statement: "Resolved, that it is the opinion of this Board that as to the general principles of liberty and the rights of man, in nature and in society, the doctrines of Locke, in his 'Essay concerning the true original extent and end of civil government,' and of Sidney in his 'Discourses on government,' may be considered as those generally approved by our fellow citizens of this, and the United States."

citizenship, where standards are now set by the Fourteenth Amendment. The other source is immigration and naturalization where standards are set by Congress.

At a particular and proper intersection of immigration and birthright citizenship, immigrants who are not yet citizens but are lawfully settled among us gained citizenship for their children — Congress in 1790 so provided. And under the Fourteenth Amendment, eligibility for birthright citizenship, for the children of immigrants who live lawfully among us, is in some instances provided by that Amendment. That citizenship comes via the Amendment's "subject to the jurisdiction" standard, as was held to be the case in *Benny v. O'Brien* and *United States v. Wong Kim Ark*. In those cases and in return for immigrant parents living among us in a lawful and peaceful manner, their children gained birthright citizenship. As reciprocity is the case — for those living lawfully among us — this entitlement to birthright citizenship is felt as right and is as such uplifting.

Birthright citizenship for immigrants here *illegally*, without the same respect for our law, is a different case. The possibilities of citizenship in this different case are examined in this and the next chapter in light of two routes, namely birthright citizenship and naturalization. Between these two routes, it is immigration and naturalization — the disregard of which has led to the whole present mess — that may offer a solution to the problem of citizenship for illegal immigrants who prove themselves deserving.

In constitutional law, citizenship cuts across a divide of "originalism." On its conservative side, originalism emphasizes abiding by the terms of the Constitution as they were understood when enacted. The liberal side is more interested in interpreting and applying these terms in light of present-day moral, social, and economic concerns. Neither side disregards the terms of the Constitution; it is just that the liberal side tends to view these terms as open-ended delegation to future generations more than does the conservative side. For citizenship, though, this divide has not held. With respect to birthright citizenship, liberals, political liberals anyway, tend to be hard-shell originalists; they interpret the Citizenship Clause of the Fourteenth Amendment strictly by what they see as the understanding of that Clause as it was enacted in 1868. By that view of the understanding, and as we have seen, citizenship is frozen to the rule of *Calvin's Case*: Place of birth alone determines citizenship and evolving moral and social conditions are disregarded. "Subject to the jurisdiction" (and the lawfulness it requires) is disregarded.

By way of illustration: As earlier noted, Great Britain, home to the *Calvin's Case*/territorial measure of birthright citizenship, displaced that measure in 1981. It did so out of rising concerns that given the mobility of today's world, people were using place of birth to gain citizenship without first being properly affiliated with the United Kingdom (as Great Britain at times now referred to itself). Accordingly and as we have seen, by its Nationality Act of 1981, the United Kingdom displaced the *Calvin's Case*/ born-within-the-kingdom rule of citizenship. It did so by providing that birthright citizenship was a right held by "British citizens" or by persons "settled in the United Kingdom." "Settled" excluded persons only temporarily present (as by "maternity tourism") within the United Kingdom. Persons within the United Kingdom in violation of immigration law were excluded as the Act provided that "a person is not to be treated . . . as ordinarily resident in the United Kingdom . . . when he is in the United Kingdom . . . in breach of the immigration laws."

Owing to a crippling originalism, though, the supposition is that we cannot act against *Calvin's Case* as did the British, because our Constitution freezes us to the place-of-birth terms of that case. The supposition is that "the ultimate practical difference between legislative curbs in the United Kingdom and the United States is that the United Kingdom can constitutionally attack territorial birthright citizenship," whereas the United States "cannot."[105] We cannot do so, it is said, in that corrective measures as we might take are precluded by the Fourteenth Amendment, because as enacted the Amendment established place of birth and just only that as a hard and fast rule. By that bad piece originalism, place of birth alone determines birthright citizenship, and Congress in light of current social, economic, and moral concerns cannot, as have the British (Ireland, India, and others), do anything about it. This is a disabling point of view, so much so that it has given rise to desperate suggestions, as by Sen. Lindsay Nelson, that the nation, in order to free itself to meet the crises at hand, the millions piling up in violation of law, had better attend to changing the Fourteenth Amendment. A point of this book is that such action — of amending the Constitution — is unnecessary. The document is not that static.

To start with, the suggestion that we change the Fourteenth Amendment to deal with illegal immigration is totally and completely wrong. It is wholly inconsistent with the Amendment's "subjection to jurisdiction" condition. For instance, had place of birth been the whole measure of birthright

---

105. Michael Robert W. Houston, Birthright Citizenship in the United Kingdom and the United States: A Comparative Analysis of the Common Law Basis for Granting Citizenship to Children Born of Illegal Immigrants, 33 *Vand. J. Transnat'l* L. 693 (2000).

citizenship, there would have been no need or occasion for a debate about a connection to the nation and its people that meet the "subject to the jurisdiction," there would have been no need to mark a distinction between being partially as opposed to fully allegiant to the nation, no cause for concern about "temporary sojourners" or of being "fully incorporated into your communities," and would have been no occasion for explaining that "subject to the jurisdiction" required a full-hearted commitment of the same "extent and quality as applies to every citizen of the of the United States." We are a republic and under the Fourteenth Amendment more than birth on our soil is essential to citizenship.

After the Fourteenth Amendment was ratified, early applications of it, in the executive branch and the courts, showed the necessity of a "substantial affiliation" with the nation. In the executive branch, Secretary of State Thomas Bayard found that German parents only temporarily present in Ohio lacked the affiliation for reasons of that impermanence. Accordingly, they were not "subject to the jurisdiction" of the United States and their child, albeit born in the United State, was not "a citizen of the United States by birth." In a different venue, of the courts, the Supreme Court in *Elk v. Wilkins* found that a person does not "merely by reason of his birth within the United States" gain citizenship and that the "evident meaning" of "subject to the jurisdiction" was "not merely subject in some respect or degree to the jurisdiction of the United States, but completely subject to their political jurisdiction, and owing them direct and immediate allegiance." Thereafter, in *Benny v. O'Brien* and *United States v. Wong Kim Ark,* the courts found that immigrants lawfully settled in the United States gained birthright citizenship for their children. In these circumstances and as the Supreme Court said, immigrants are "in so many respects situated similarly to citizens." They were in fact "subject to the jurisdiction."

For those immigrants, the relevant metrics first of all sound in reciprocity. The children of *legal* immigrants gained birthright citizenship *in return* for their parents' allegiance. That relation, of "allegiance and obedience to the laws," was in fact a stock phrase in debate on the Fourteenth Amendment. Second of all, the Amendment requires faithfulness to the country. Illegal immigrants, though, often assume a contrary power of movement back and forth between Mexico and the United States, as they wish and in evasion in violation of their duty to the nation. During my writing of this book, the Atlanta Journal Constitution had an account of an illegal immigrant back in court on a fifth conviction; one of the prior convictions was for a hit and run that killed an elderly person. The offender had moved back and forth across the border, evading accountability for his multiple offenses. As said by the district attorney the case was not all exceptional, "We deal with it every day."[106] As illegal immigrants reserve for themselves the power to go back and forth across borders as they wish, they put themselves into the class of "temporary sojourners" identified in deliberations on the Fourteenth Amendment as persons of no enduring commitment to the United States and who are ineligible for citizenship.

Past their initial breach of allegiance, that of disregarding immigration standards, the notion is that illegal immigrants have yet become deserving, by thereafter living responsibly and lawfully among us. The one response to this thought is that it cannot be right: The Fourteenth Amendment is as is, and as it is the Amendment does not provide birthright citizenship for persons who have so primarily breached the law—imigration law—that preserves citizenship.

But assume that is not the case; assume that past that breach and by afterwards living responsibly in the manner of citizens, illegal immigrants might yet qualify for birthright citizenship. Illegal immigrants do not qualify. Whether those unlawfully within the country have then lived in the manner of citizens, the problem is: Who's to say? They are not subject to military service, they pay or may not pay taxes, they may or may not contribute to social security, they may or may not contribute to public goods such as welfare, and again—who is to say? Whether illegal immigrants are so connected to us and the nation is a matter that is obscured and evaded. Consequently, we have no way of knowing whether they have assumed the contributive responsibilities of citizens. We cannot know the extent they have used us as opposed to casting their lots with us.

A number of illegal immigrants do live here in a manner that approximates that of committed and contributing citizens. The problem, however, are those others who have not. According to a 2005 Bear Stearns study on our underground economy, "approximately 5 million illegal workers are collecting wages on a cash basis and are avoiding income taxes." For Los Angeles County in 2004, the Economic Roundtable, a nonprofit research organization in a meticulously prepared study, found that the underground economy generated by the illegal immigrants "added up to over $2 billion in unpaid payroll benefits and insurance that were needed to fund a minimal social safety net for workers." *Enforcement actions* brought by Immigration and Customs Enforcement (ICE) provide some substantiation of these evasions. ICE actions are against firms involved in money laundering. They act as intermediaries that facilitate cash payments from employers to illegal workers, and such cash exchanges avoid social security taxes and state and federal income taxes as might be paid by workers

---

106. *Atlanta Journal Constitution*, Aug. 2010, A-1, 5th Column.

and employers.[107] These nondisclosures by illegal immigrants allow for evasion of civic responsibilities in a way uncharacteristic of citizens or of lawfully settled immigrants.

As they have avoided contributing their fair share to the creation of public goods, a number of illegal immigrants have drawn from those goods by claiming benefits such as education. The amount drawn down, from the federal government and the states, is significant.[108] The fact of those withdrawals, however, is not the point. Rather, the point and principle is that the undocumented status of recipients allows them to take these benefits unfairly, by avoiding corresponding responsibilities such as taxes, and there is evidence that a number of them do so. As this happens, it is exploitation. "Citizens have the right" that you pay a fair share; they "have the right to expect you to make this effort. Failure to do so treats them in an offensively instrumental way; or, as we more usually say, it exploits them".[109]

These failures, of allegiance and of nondisclosure, cut against an entitlement to birthright citizenship to illegal immigrants under the Fourteenth Amendment. These things considered, for persons unlawfully present in the United States, a constitutional right to birthright citizenship is at best a hard case. I am not alone in saying so. The conclusion reached by Professors Schuck and Smith in their book on *Citizenship Without Consent* (1985) is that "automatic political membership for the native-born children of illegal aliens seems difficult to defend, especially when access to citizenship

---

107. Robert Justich & Betty Ng, CFA, The Underground Labor Force is Rising to the Surface (Bear Stearns, January 3, 2005); Hopeful Workers, Marginal Jobs: LA's Off-the-Books Labor Force, Economic Round Table, available at www.economicrt.org; ICE Financial Investigation Initiative Combats Illegal Worker Employment, available at www.ice.gov/doclib/news/library/reports. The Economic Round Table report also identifies an additional means of tax evasion, saying that the undocumented "in Los Angeles County spend an estimated $4.1 billion per year that should generate $440 million in sales tax revenue. However these workers purchase many goods and services from informal retailers and service providers who do not collect sales taxes and submit them to the state".

108. Although the amount unlawful immigrants drawn down is significant, estimates of it vary. One such account is by Steven Camarota, The High Cost of Cheap Labor: Illegal Immigration and the Federal Budget (Center for Immigration Studies: 2004). A more recent account is provided by the Federation for Immigration Study's 2013 report on "The Fiscal Burden of Illegal Immigration on United States Taxpayers", available at www.fairus.org/publications/the-fiscal-burden-of-illegal-immigration-on-united-states-taxpayers

109. White, The Civic Minimum, *supra*, at 62.

for other needy groups must be limited."[110] But there is a different route, apart from the Fourteenth Amendment, for some of them.

The Fourteenth Amendment stands among the Constitution's "majestic generalities." These generalities, broadly stated to endure over time, yet need be infused with clarity and bite by means of implementing rules. Otherwise they stand to lapse into dormancy, as the Fourteenth Amendment may now be doing. But with an authoritative set of implementing "rules" (and I mean just that, rules) at hand, we can finally and confidently address the matter of birthright citizenship as opposed to being paralyzed by uncertainty about it as we now are. The need for rules by which birthright citizenship can be properly and effectively applied is the requirement, but the question arises which institutions is best suited and sited to provide them.

That institution is Congress. To an extent the courts might themselves do so, if and as appropriate sets of facts are brought to them. But while the courts can decide instances of citizenship as they are presented, on the whole their process seems suboptimal, at least in comparison to Congress. Congress is better suited to working through the complex of social, economic, ecological, and moral issues that citizenship entails. It has broad-based decisional processes that the courts lack. Also, Congress does not have to await the appropriate case, it can act proactively. It has the power, especially it has power, to do so.

As the nation finally attends to sorting through the circumstances of illegal immigrants, it may turn out persons not entitled to citizenship under the Fourteenth Amendment can otherwise gain citizenship if a special path is opened. Congress can provide the path by a power the Constitution vests only in it. The power comes out Section 5 of the Fourteenth Amendment. The power is there, but it has never been used for citizenship. That power is the subject of the next chapter.

---

110. *See also* Lino A. Graglia, Birthright Citizenship for Children of Illegal Aliens: An Irrational. Public Policy, 14 *Tex. Rev. L. & Pol.* 1 (2009); John C. Eastman, Heritage Foundation, From Feudalism to Consent: Rethinking Birthright Citizenship (2006), available at www.heritage.org/Research

# Chapter Nine

# Congressional Power

"It is a legitimate concern of Congress that those who bear
American citizenship and receive its benefits have some
nexus to the United States."

Rogers v. Bellei, 401 U.S. 815, 832 (1971)

Within a republic, living well entails respect, a self and mutual respect
that is a reinforcing part of a citizen. Such respect is formed out of a personal
commitment to living responsibly, to others as well as to oneself, and the confidence
that this commitment is shared by others. With this respect, coherence
and cohesion fortified by moral sensibility is possible. This possibility
was identified at Athens as living well, and thereafter realized in North
America, as said in James Kettner's account of the citizen, of "Americans
mov[ing] toward a new understanding of the ties that bound individuals
into the community." Maintenance of these ties is particularly done by Congress.
That body "ensures[s] some tie between this country and one who
seeks citizenship."[111]

Citizenship ought to be a prime site for Congress to ensure those ties. Congress
has the power and resources that other parts of the government, courts
included, do not have. It can lay down a set of rules for which — owing to the
clarity rules bring — there are crying needs.

But first and as to resources, Congress has decisional processes better
suited to the multifaceted problems associated with the citizen than do the
courts. It can do comprehensive studies where courts, restricted by rules

---

111. James H. Kettner, The Idea of Volitional Allegiance, 18 *Am. J. Legal Hist.* 208,
219 (1974). *See* Tuan Anh Nguyen v. Immigration and Naturalization Service, 533 U.S.
53, 68 (2001).

of evidence, a sense of justiciable issues, and with limited staffs, cannot. Congress has a good range of remedies, proactive as well as reactive, and it can set them in place, visibly and accessibly by legislation. Also, Congress has a better connection with citizens. Congress can hear from them on a county-to-county basis. And in these matters the citizenry need be heard, its vitality is at stake. An engaged Congress might usefully do three things respecting the citizenry. First, it can better hear citizens. Second, it can add clarity by specifying, after sifting through complex circumstances, those who are entitled to citizenship and those who are not. Third, as Congress finds that this specification is in some circumstances unfair, it can provide a certain relief. The first two of these things are the power of Congress, by Section 5 of the Fourteenth Amendment. The third is by Congress under its power of naturalization.

# Section 5

As the Fourteenth Amendment sets a good connection with the country as the condition necessary to birthright citizenship, it does so by the broad spectrum standard of "subject to the jurisdiction." Fully to be effective, a standard of this breadth needs to be implemented through rules. As said, it is no exception that without the clarity and bite of rules, standards of this sort tend to lapse to unenforced ambiguity and "subject to the jurisdiction" is one of them. Here we lack answers to even easy questions, as whether vacationing parents from abroad are entitled to birthright citizenship. A harder question is about illegal immigrants. Without answers, "subject to the jurisdiction" goes unenforced.

The benefit if not the necessity of implementing "subject to the jurisdiction" by rules issued by Congress is recognized by the Fourteenth Amendment itself. In its last section, Section 5, the Amendment provides, "The Congress shall have power to enforce, by appropriate legislation, the provisions of this article." In reference to Section 5, Sen. Charles Sumner of Massachusetts in 1868 cited Congress's authority "to enforce this definition of Citizenship . . . by appropriate legislation." As well, Senator Howard explained that Section 5 "casts upon Congress the responsibility of seeing to it, for the future, that all the sections of the amendment are carried out in good faith." The Supreme Court has explained that Section 5 gave Congress this elevated power, saying "it is the power of Congress which has been enlarged" and enlarged toward the end of making the Amendment "fully effective."[112]

---

112. Ex parte Virginia, 100 U.S. 339, 345 (1879). *See also* Katzenbach v. Morgan, 384 U.S. 641, 649 ff (1966). Sen. Charles Summers' remarks are at 14 *The Works of Charles*

For birthright citizenship, however, Congress has not exercised its Section 5 power, it never has. Presently the US Code, at 8 United States Code Sec. 1401(a), provides that "a person born in the United States, and subject to the jurisdiction thereof" gains birthright citizenship. This is a simple repetition of the Amendment's terms; the statute is *not* a rule interpreting the terms of the Amendment. In the manner of interpretation what is now needed, in light of modern travel and massive movements of people, is a specification of "subject to the jurisdiction" by means of rules. Under Section 5 what might the specifications — the rules that Congress might make — be? For starters, children born in the United States to citizen parents are of course born as citizens. The child's tie to the parents as a matter of course inculcates citizenship. Another rule is that children born in the United States to lawfully settled immigrants are born as citizens. (But only to *legal* immigrants who are in fact resident.) Moreover, debate on the Fourteenth Amendment established that children born here to parents from abroad could not be citizens. Congress should by rule now make clear that those children–born here to parents from abroad–do not gain birthright citizenship.

Deference as owed Congress comes out of Section 5's placement of the power to enforce the Fourteenth Amendment in that institution, out of a regard for Congress's decisional resources, and out of history as it is evidence of a legislative competency to which the courts may accede. Out of history, in the words of Supreme Court Justice Felix Frankfurter, "is not merely a page of history . . . but a whole volume." In 1790 Congress provided citizenship, upon their parents' naturalization, to the children of immigrants. In the Civil Rights Act of 1866, Congress provided the first general definition of birthright citizenship. Thereafter, Congress drafted and approved the "born in the United States and subject to the jurisdiction thereof'" terms of the Fourteenth Amendment. In 1924 and through a special power respecting Native Americans, Congress provided they were entitled to birthright citizenship irrespective of tribal affiliation. Today, Congress constantly attends to birthright citizenship for children born abroad to US citizens, modifying the law (which was enacted in 1790) to keep pace with changing responsibilities of marriage and parents and assuring that ties of parent and child to the nation are maintained.

These things, the Fourteenth Amendment's specific delegation of enforcement power to Congress, Congress's decisional resources, and a history of congressional action respecting citizenship, provide a following wind. As

---

Sumner 385 (1883) and Senator Howard's remarks at Cong. Globe, 39th Cong., 1st Sess. Generally *see* Flack, *The Adoption of the Fourteenth Amendment* 138ff (1908).

was the case in *Katzenbach v. Morgan*. This was a Supreme Court decision about an attribute of citizenship, of participation in political processes, for persons of Puerto Rican origin. Under Section 5 of the Fourteenth Amendment, Congress had waived, for voting by persons educated in Puerto Rican schools, certain English literacy requirements. Because that waiver was inconsistent with New York law that state challenged it, claiming the waiver was outside Congress's Section 5 power. The state argued that the enactment "can only be sustained if the judicial branch determines that the state law is prohibited by the provisions of the Amendment that Congress sought to enforce."

In other words, the argument was that Congress had no independent authority to determine the content of the Fourteenth Amendment; instead, Congress had to rely on court determinations of that content and then legislate accordingly. The Court, though, rejected the argument, saying that such a secondary role for Congress "would depreciate both congressional resourcefulness and congressional responsibility for implementing the Amendment." That being the case, the Court's own part was "not to determine whether the New York English literacy requirement . . . violates the Equal Protection Clause." But instead to determine whether the congressional determination at issue was "appropriate, that is, adapted to carry out the objects" the Amendment had in view.

For illegal immigrants in this country today, birthright citizenship under the Fourteenth Amendment requires more than place of birth; the "subject to the jurisdiction" measure of the Amendment must be met. In debate on the Amendment, a point made was that any person within the United States is "entitled . . . to the protection of the laws." But with a grain of salt. As said by Senator Williams, "In one sense, all persons born within the territorial limits of the United States are subject to the jurisdiction of the United States, but they are not subject to the jurisdiction of the United States in every sense. . . . I understand the words here, subject to the jurisdiction of the United States to mean fully and completely subject to the jurisdiction of the United States." A person must be completely "subject to the jurisdiction" and "within the protection of the law" is an element of the jurisdiction.

As this connection — of "subject to the jurisdiction" — is the case, the question is: What are the qualities of the connection? As identified by ordinary means of constitutional interpretation, by the terms, history, and context of the "subject to the jurisdiction," these qualities are an enduring allegiance and commitment to the nation and an assumption of contributive responsibilities in the manner of citizens. As Congress may identify such qualities, that determination, owing to that institution's particular competency and history considering the composition of our citizenry, stands to carry some weight.

About that weight, it includes what Justice Harlan in *Katzenbach v. Morgan* referred to as "legislative facts." Any number of constitutionally protected values rest on "empirical foundations." These foundations Harlan spoke of as legislative facts and of them "Congress is well equipped to investigate" and congressional determinations thus made are "entitled to due respect." "Well equipped" by virtue of capacities for democratic representation and for comprehensive study as Congress has done the work. As Congress brings its capacities to bear, as it does the work, and as it may study, deliberate, and reach conclusions regarding those persons who meet the qualities of connection set by the Fourteenth Amendment, its conclusions are entitled to due respect.

As in *Tuan Anh Nguyen v. Immigration and Naturalization Service*: This case involved 8 U.S.C. 1409(a) and by it Congress's adjustment, for children born out of wedlock, to the original 1790 enactment providing citizenship to children born abroad to US citizens. The adjustment required a special showing, on the part of the father, of a relation between him and the child. For present purposes, the details of that relation are not important. However, Congress's reasons for requiring that relation are important. As noted by the courts, Congress required a "double" relation, an association of the father with the United States and then of the father with child, so that the child might absorb the father's civic character. As the Court succinctly stated, this association was "one that consists of the real, everyday ties that provide a connection between child and citizen parent and, in turn, the United States." In *Tuan Anh Nguyen* the Court credited congressional power respecting the necessity and quality of those ties, noting Congress might properly "ensure some tie between this country and one who seeks citizenship" and that as to "the realities of the child's own ties and allegiances, it is for Congress and not this Court, to make that determination."[113] For these reasons, of ties and allegiance and Congress's capacity to determine them, the courts will defer to Congress as it may, by Section 5 rules for birthright citizenship as it may issue, bring that capacity to bear as rules of connection with the nation.

# Naturalization

Illegal immigrants do not gain birthright citizenship under the Fourteenth Amendment. They are here illegally. Yet Congress may find that

---

113. Tuan Anh Nguyen v. Immigration and Naturalization Service, 533 U.S. at 53, 67–68, 83–84 (2001).

some of them are eligible for citizenship, but by another route. By means of its Article I, Section 8 power over naturalization, Congress can provide this different route.

Congress by its power over naturalization can open a channel to citizenship, exactly how can it do so for illegal immigrants? First of all with care, an example of is proved by the Immigration Reform and Control Act of 1986 by which Congress did indeed provide a route to citizenship for illegal immigrants. That Act's success was making amnesty a bad word. Its failure, though, was in not meeting the goal, stated by President Reagan, of "preserv[ing] the value of one of the most sacred possessions of our people: American citizenship."

The 1986 Act was less than a full-hearted effort. Of its enactment it was said, "Everyone was sort of holding their nose, blocking their eyes, doing the best that could get cobbled together." And that proved to be not much: The Act's not very rigorous provisions were showed a lack of conviction about citizenship, as did the fraud tolerated in enforcing the Act' provisions as they were. Documentation, for instance of an applicant living continuously within the United States as opposed to moving back and forth across the border, was often false. The Act's provisions against employers of illegal labor were not much enforced. Consequently, disregard of immigration law and unfair competition, by firms employing illegal aliens and paying lower wages and avoiding taxes, continued.

And just so, illegal immigration ticked upward to modern levels. A number of illegal immigrants did not seek amnesty under the Act and may not have wanted it as it required documentation from them and their visibility for purposes of taxes. Those who did gain amnesty provided a better point of contact for a new wave of illegal immigrants. As illegal entries thus prospered immigration seems to have suffered; illegal immigrants came to outnumber legal immigrants as much as by three to one.

Against that background of failure, how should Congress now act? Perhaps by beginning with the study ordered by Congress and done under a commission led by Barbara Jordan of Texas. The report of that commission, issued under the heading of *U.S. Immigration Policy: Restoring Credibility* (1994), was that "The Commission believes it is essential to control illegal immigration if we are to have a credible immigration policy. We believe legal immigration is in the national interest, but see illegal immigration as a threat both to our long tradition of immigration and to our commitment to the rule of law."

Where Congress might act, and do so fairly and without diminishing the values emphasized by the Jordan commission, is to act for persons who themselves have *not* willingly violated immigration law. These persons would be children brought here or born here and who have not purposefully breached those laws. In many cases, these children may have an established life here, among schools and friends, and have assimilated into our culture so that their removal is a hardship. Accordingly, for them another way to citizenship may be in order. As mentioned, France provided a model. By the Méhaignerie Act of 1993, France provided for birthright citizenship but only to its citizens. However, for children born in France to persons who were not citizens, that Act provides a different tract to citizenship. By this route those children might, if they so elected and after meeting certain qualifications, become French citizens as they became of age. Our Congress can do likewise.

But then, what about the illegal immigrants who do willfully violate immigration law? By its Article I, Section 8 power over naturalization, Congress also opens a route to citizenship for them. But, as we said, it should be done carefully. A number of illegal immigrants are criminals, murders done by them flash across the screen. Congress certainly will not provide them a route to citizenship. But what about the rest, who, apart from illegally entering the country, are not criminals? What Congress does or does not for them is then the issue. For at least twenty-five years, Congress has done nothing. As debates on the 2016 presidential elections have shown, it should now act. But that action, if it comes, will be hard.

The cost of sending millions back across the border is significant. Estimates are about ten thousand dollars per person. On the other hand, there are the costs that illegal immigrants impose on us. Illegal immigrants do not serve in the armed forces, so our citizens must serve for them. Education for the children of illegal immigrants is paid by the states. Some illegal immigrants do pay social security and Medicare taxes but others do not. Some do go back and forth across the border and are but "temporary sojourners" in this country. Illegal immigrants do have jobs, but often neither they nor their employers pay taxes. These jobs gained cut against jobs held by citizens who do pay.

Action must now be taken, but it is the work of Congress. It has contacts with the people and has committees to sort through the work, statistics and all, to separate those must be sent back from those who stay here. Those who do stay must be tested same as legal immigrants are, for language and civic skills. This selection for illegal immigrants must now be done. Eleven million people here illegally are not a cost we can carry. As well, people here illegally must now identify themselves, otherwise we are back to where we started in 1986 as people just keep coming over the border.

At times, illegal immigrants use their children as chips for their placement in our nation. ("Anchor babies" is the common name.) In a number of cases, parents claim citizenship for children born here and then argue that their, the parents, deportation amounts to a "constructive deportation" of the child or an undue hardship on the child as the child remains in the United States. Uniformly, these claims are rejected. In *Coleman v. United States* a parent faced deportation. She, the parent, was here unlawfully (she had been previously deported and had illegally reentered) and was using a forged social security card. In defense, she claimed that her deportation would be a "constructive deportation" of her "citizen child" as she the parent was deported.

The parent claimed her child was a citizen owing to his birth in the United States. Just for purposes of its decision, the court accepted that claim as true. Nonetheless, the court found that claims about the child's constructive deportation were not a defense against the parent's deportation. In so ruling the court noted that those claims had been denied by the decision of every court that had considered them.[114]

One of those decisions was that of the Seventh Circuit Court of Appeals in *Oforji v. Ashcroft*, where Judge Posner entered a notable concurrence,

---

114. Coleman v. United States, 454 F.Supp.2d 757 (N.D. Ill., 2006). Diaz v. Kay-Dix Ranch, 9 Cal.App.3d. 588 (1970) is a similar case. It was brought early on in the struggle against illegal labor and was brought by legal farmworkers. Their allegation was that "defendants' unlawful practice of hiring illegal entrants denies plaintiffs and their class work opportunities which would otherwise be available, increases the rate of unemployment and depresses the earnings of Northern California farmworkers; that the hiring of illegal entrants cost Northern California farmworkers approximately $2,700,000 in lost wages in 1969 and costs the public increased annual welfare expenditures of not less than $1,400,000 for the support of domestic farmworkers and their families." Plaintiffs then asked the court to enjoin defendants' hiring of illegal workers, in that it was unfair competition under California law.

The court agreed, noting that the complained of practice "undermines the standards American workers generally enjoy throughout the rest of the country" and that "the normal play of free enterprise principles is subverted." Be that as it may be, the court did not grant the relief, of an injunctive against the continued hiring of illegal workers. Such relief, the court said, would be futile owing to what the court referred to as the "misfeasance" of federal officials. By misfeasance, the court meant that while the federal government had taken center stage in these matters of illegal immigration violations, the government best played a lackluster role. In the courts' words:

A paradox of this lawsuit is plaintiff's discerned need for a decree compelling inquiry by California farm operators when an agency of the federal government — supplied with an apparatus of offices, staff and computerized equipment — is unwilling or unable to conduct that inquiry. Plaintiffs seek the aid of equity because the national government has breached the commitment implied by national immigration policy. It is more orderly, more effectual, less burdensome to the affected interests, that the national government redeems its commitment. Thus the court of equity withholds its aid.

notable as it included an appeal to Congress to dispel the confusion about whether illegal immigrants were entitled to birthright citizenship. Judge Posner wrote:

> This rule [birthright citizenship for illegal immigrants] thought by some to be compelled by section 1 of the Fourteenth Amendment . . . makes no sense. . . . Congress would not be flouting the Constitution if it amended the Immigration and Nationality Act to put an end to the nonsense. On May 5, 2003, H.R. 1567, a bill "To amend the Immigration and Nationality Act to deny citizenship at birth to children born in the United States of parents who are not citizens or permanent resident aliens," was referred to the House Subcommittee on Immigration, Border Security, and Claims. I hope it passes.[115]

---

115. Oforji v. Ashcroft, 354 F.3d 609, 621–22 (7th Cir. 2003).

# Conclusion

*The sustainers* are our citizens. In the early sixteenth century, we began to work toward being a republic nation. We started it at Jamestown and Plymouth and kept at it until the 1770s when it all came together. Before 1776, there was no word for us; we were only the "subjects" of Great Britain. But in 1776, we found the right word, *citizen*. On July 4, 1776, we used the word for the first time in public document, the document being the Declaration of Independence. Thereafter, citizen was used ten times in the Constitution of 1787, but the word was not yet fully formed. In 1787, we knew who the first citizens were; they were "We the People" specified in the first sentence of the Constitution. But who were the next generations, were they also citizens? Of course, a short time after 1787 and for descendants of "We the People," our answer was that they too were citizens.

This identification of the citizen, though, had a critical fault. It did not include African Americans, did not include them at all. See, for instance, the *Dred Scott v. Sandford* case. For that reason, we fought the Civil War and enacted the Fourteenth Amendment. The Amendment provides citizenship to African Americans. They are included, as we all are, by the Amendment's first two words of "All persons." With that opener, the Amendment provides that "All persons born or naturalized in the United States, and subject to the jurisdiction thereof, are citizens of the United States and of the state wherein they reside."

In that sentence, "All persons" is followed by two conditions. The first condition is a geographic nexus, of "born . . . in the United States." The second condition is a matter of relationship, stated as "subject to the jurisdiction." This second condition has a history, which began with Chancellor Kent's use of the phrase in *Goodell v. Jackson* to mean not only must persons who were born in the nation but also "form[ed] a part of the body politic, or people of the state." That history is shown in debate on the Fourteenth Amendment, that to be a citizen a person must be in and connected to community, state, and nation.

In the 1890s, our courts found that children born to immigrants—here legally—met both conditions, of birth on our soil and "subject to the jurisdiction," of the Amendment. The immigrant parents were living lawfully and peacefully and thus their children gained birthright citizenship under the Amendment. The obverse of those decisions is that the Amendment does not apply to immigrants who are here *illegally*.

Today millions of people in the United States are *not* citizens. They cannot be; they are illegal immigrants. That problem has escalated and that for some reason or the other our politicians now ignore it. A number of those here illegally are in fact criminals, and we know we should send them back over the border or to wherever they came from. But mostly we don't, we suffer the crime. For the remainder, there is the cost, perhaps ten thousand dollars or more per person, to deport them. But there are also costs in letting them stay here, the costs I have covered as best I can.

But there is a humanitarian issue to consider as well, that is, those who are in fact here illegally but not by their own fault. They are the children of illegal immigrants. These children cannot be citizens, not by the Fourteenth Amendment, but they do need a break. Congress can do that by opening a way, by naturalization under Article I, Section 8, to make them a citizen. As to the rest of those here illegally, they cannot claim their illegal status is not their fault. Their status is up to Congress.

As said at the beginning this book, it is about becoming a citizen. The citizen is necessary, and thus the book ends with the quote so much used, made in 1787 and there outside the Constitution hall, that ours is "A republic if you can keep it."